D0947167

LUIGI
PIRANDELLO

WORLD DRAMATISTS

In the same series:

Edward Albee	*Ronald Hayman*
Samuel Beckett	*Ronald Hayman*
Calderón	*Heinz Gerstinger*
Anton Chekhov	*Siegfried Melchinger*
Euripides	*Siegfried Melchinger*
Henrik Ibsen	*Hans Georg Meyer*
Arthur Miller	*Ronald Hayman*
Molière	*Gertrud Mander*
John Osborne	*Ronald Hayman*
Harold Pinter	*Ronald Hayman*
Arthur Schnitzler	*Reinhard Urbach*
Sophocles	*Siegfried Melchinger*
Lope de Vega and Spanish Drama	*Heinz Gerstinger*
August Strindberg	*Gunnar Ollén*
Arnold Wesker	*Ronald Hayman*

WORLD DRAMATISTS

LUIGI PIRANDELLO

RENATE MATTHAEI

Translated by Simon and Erika Young

WITH HALFTONE ILLUSTRATIONS

FREDERICK UNGAR PUBLISHING CO.
NEW YORK

Translated, and adapted, from the German.
Published by arrangement with Friedrich Verlag,
Velber, Germany.

CONTENTS

Chronology   1
Pirandello's Life and Work   5
    1. Sicily   5
    2. Fascism   10
    3. Sicilian Dialect Theater and
       the Theater of the Grotesque   18
    4. The Plays on the Stage   26
Plays   33
    Cap and Bells   33
    Thus It Is (If It Seems So to You)   43
    The Pleasure of Honesty   68
    Six Characters in Search of an Author   76
    Henry IV   102
    To Clothe the Naked   118
    Each in His Own Way   129
    Tonight We Improvise   143
    The Mountain Giants   154
Bibliography   169
Index   177

CHRONOLOGY

1867	Luigi Pirandello is born on 28 June in Agrigento, Sicily, the son of Stefano Pirandello, owner of sulfur mines.
1881	The Pirandello family moves to Palermo, where Luigi attends the gymnasium.
1883	His first poems are published.
1884	*Capanetta* (Little Huts), written in the verismo style, is published.
1886	He graduates from the gymnasium and starts to study law and philosophy at the University of Palermo. Writes his first drama, *Birds That Fly High*.
1887–89	He continues his studies in Rome. Writes *Mal giocondo* (Painful Joy), a volume of poetry.
1889–91	Continues his studies in Bonn.
1890	Translates Goethe's *Römische Elegien* into Italian.
1891	Receives his degree in Bonn with a dissertation on sounds and development of sound in the dialect of Agrigento.

For the reader's convenience, all play titles are given in English. Please see the bibliography for original titles and translation information.

1892	Teaches Italian and Italian literature in Bonn. Returns to Rome, where he is active as a freelance writer. Forms a friendship with verismo writers Luigi Capuana and Ugo Fleres.
1893	Publishes his first novel, *L'esclusa* (The Outcast).
1894	Failure of socialist uprising in Sicily, in which Pirandello took part. Marries Antonietta Portulano.
1896	Publishes the drama *If Not So, or Other People's Reasons*.
1898–1921	Becomes assistant professor at the Istituto Superiore de Magisterio, teaching Italian literature.
1904	*Il fu Mattia Pascal* (The Late Mattia Pascal), a novel, is published. He loses his fortune because a flood destroys the sulfur mines. His wife suffers a nervous breakdown. Writing becomes a means of making a living.
1908	Publishes the novel *I vecchi e i giovani* (The Old and the Young) and an essay on humor. The play *The Vise* is published.
1909	Publishes the novel *Su marito* (Her Husband).
1910	Two of his plays, *Sicilian Limes* and *The Vise*, are given their premieres in Rome.
1916	*Think, Giacomino!* is premiered in Rome, and one of his plays for the Sicilian dialect theater, *Liolà*, has its premiere in Rome. Pirandello publishes the play *Cap and Bells*.
1917	*Thus It Is (If It Seems So to You)* is

premiered in Milan, *The Pleasure of Honesty* is premiered in Turin, and *Cap and Bells* is premiered in Rome.

1918   *Role Playing* is premiered in Rome.

1919   Pirandello's wife is committed to a sanatarium for nervous disorder. *Man, Beast, and Virtue* is premiered in Milan.

1920   *As Well as Before, Better than Before* is premiered in Venice, and *Mrs. Morli, One and Two* is premiered in Rome.

1921   *Six Characters in Search of an Author* is premiered in Rome.

1922   The play *Henry IV* is published and premiered in Milan, and *To Clothe the Naked* is premiered in Rome.

1922–37   *Novelle per un anno* (A Novel per Year) is published in 15 volumes.

1923   The play *Each in His Own Way* is published.

1924   *Each in His Own Way* is premiered in Milan. Pirandello becomes a member of the fascist party.

1925   He begins his own theater company, the Teatro d'Arte di Roma, which receives a subsidy from the state. The theater opens with *The Festival of Our Lord of the Ship*, and Mussolini attends the performance. Pirandello tours with his troupe in England, France, Germany, and America.

1926   Mussolini asks him to submit a plan for a national theater. He tours Austria.

1927   He tours South America.

1928   His theater troupe breaks up because of lack of money. *The New Colony* is premiered in Rome.

1929	Becomes a member of the newly established Accademia d'Italia. The play *Tonight We Improvise* and the opera libretto *The Fable of the Changeling Son* are published.
1930	*Tonight We Improvise* is premiered in Königsberg, Germany.
1933	He goes on lecture tours through Scandinavia and Latin America.
1934	*The Fable of the Changeling Son*, an opera, is premiered in Braunschweig, Germany, and Hitler attends the performance. Pirandello receives the Nobel Prize for Literature.
1936	*The Mountain Giants* is published. Pirandello dies of pneumonia on 10 December.
1937	*The Mountain Giants* is premiered in Florence.

PIRANDELLO'S LIFE AND WORK

1. Sicily

"Each one must arrange his mask as best he can—his outer mask. For inside of it there is then the inner mask, which often fails to square with the outer. And nothing is true!" Thus wrote Pirandello in 1908 in his important essay on humor (*L'umorismo*). And this idea lies at the root of all his plays, which he called collectively *maschere nude* (naked masks). What he was concerned with in this work was nothing but the constant assembling and dismantling of the personality in the struggle of life.

Pirandello's attitude to life was one of fear—fear of others, fear of himself and his own hard-to-control emotionality, fear of the demands made by society and fear of isolation, fear of the bewildered emptiness of a mind that has come to know the fragility of all accepted norms and categories. There is no way out of this world of fear, only rushed improvisation and refuge in momentary adaptations, adaptations that immediately fall asunder because of the excessive pres-

sures of convention and the inrush of élan vital anar-
chically gone astray.

This pattern of behavior, from which Pirandello's
characters derive their dramatic impetus, has for him
a quality of immutability, of permanence. Italian bourgeois society at the turn of the century became in his
plays the universal world stage, lying outside history
and demonstrating with abstract inevitability the ever
same message—the impossibility of communication in
an absurdly organized world. Pirandello never quite
realized, or he put out of his mind, the fact that this
world was primarily the world of Sicily, with its special historical and social conditions. For Sicily had
left its mark on him so early, and had so afflicted him
with the traumas of an authoritarian society, that he
could never even in later life see the Sicilian situation
in perspective. The small-town life of Sicily, with all
the excesses engendered by an oppressively rigid system, remained for him always a symbol of profound
metaphysical disturbance.

Pirandello's earliest years were spent in Agrigento, a
small Sicilian port, whose way of life had remained
unaltered for generations. This island life was monot-
onous and rigidly ordered, dictated by a caste system
that imposed strictly ritualized mores. Ideas from outside filtered in only slowly. Economic development,
paralyzed in an anachronism that blocked any change
in mental attitudes, lagged centuries behind that of
the continent.

"The Sicily in which Pirandello grew up," wrote his
biographer Gaspare Giudice, "was a place in which
history moved slowly, despite Italy's unification. The
system of the latifundia and the existence of feudal

customs were the basis of social life to a far greater extent than they are today. Conditions of work in the sulphur industry were still organized on medieval lines. The caste system, more complex than one would think, was capable of only superficial change, for its structures were inflexible."

The way life was lived in this backward, rigidly controlled provincial society encouraged suppressed violence, which often erupted abruptly, and secrecy. The passionate Sicilian temperament tended to find release in impulsive acts—in adultery, dueling, and murder. At night Pirandello heard the cries of duelists confronting each other in the lane behind his father's house. He experienced his father's violent rages, and surprised him one day with a mistress. On another occasion, in a mortuary that he had entered out of curiosity, he watched two people making love alongside a bier on which a dead person lay—an experience that horrified him above all others.

This was the secretive, distorted, taboo-ridden life of an authoritarian society, one projecting the facade of a stagnating status quo; of the sleepy boredom of provincial life, where any deviation from the norm was pursued by gossip and character assassination, where curiosity spied on everyone.

The sinister ambiguity of Sicilian life must have meant great insecurity and terror for an unusually sensitive boy like the young Pirandello. This quality was especially strong in his immediate milieu, first and foremost in the figure of his father, and later, when he had left childhood behind him, in that of his psychotic wife.

Both were typical products of Sicilian society. The

father, "a bear of a man, over six feet tall, with a long black beard growing down to the middle of his chest, with piercing eyes, a mighty nose, and an inflexible character, capable of terrifying attacks of rage," had a keen awareness of his standing as the prosperous owner of a sulphur business. He was as violent as he was touchy, was involved in several duels, and tangled with the Mafia. At home he ruled with all the despotism of a patriarch. He expected unconditional respect and obedience. Any opposition was punished with furious anger or a silence lasting for months.

It was not possible, Pirandello later remembered, to ask him anything or to talk with him. This deprivation of personal contact, which was coexisting with a continuous threat, was a heavy psychological burden for Pirandello, who was a child in need of affection and communication.

Shortly before his death he wrote:

> I remember how I always believed from early childhood on that I could communicate with anyone. This was naive of me, and led to bitter disappointment. But it also led me to refine my powers of expression and to feel the need to study others in order to inform myself about the nature of those with whom I was dealing. All this, however, was accompanied by the unshakable faith that I could express myself to all of them about everything. And I may say that I have worked to this end from that time on. As a boy I even had difficulties talking with my mother. As to my father, it seemed impossible— not only when I was preparing myself to talk with him but in the actual attempts, which usu-

ally ended in abysmal failure. As a writer I have much to be grateful to him for, on account of the frantic anxieties of those moments.

Pirandello's vacillations between repression and aggression, and his nervous language, which keeps coming to a halt, disintegrates, starts afresh, and cannot finish, seem to have had their origin in his traumatic relationship with his father. This same difficulty of communication was later to be repeated with his wife, who, like him, was a victim of Sicilian upbringing. The daughter of a father who was given to pathological attacks of jealousy, who locked all windows, allowed no one to enter the house, and demanded that she cross the street with bowed head and lowered eyes, she was incapable of responding to Pirandello's fierce craving for communication. The marriage, arranged in the traditional style by the two fathers who were business friends, became a torture to both. Increasingly there developed in Pirandello's wife that breakdown in communication that is the symptom of paranoia. Like her father, she became prey to a jealousy that turned into persecution mania. She lay in wait for her husband, watched his every move, scrutinized what he spent and what he said. The fear that had been suppressed for so many years broke out in terrible scenes, which Pirandello sought in vain to soothe. Every attempt at explanation, at refuting her wild accusations, only served to increase her distrust.

The never-ending effort to come to an understanding became a meaningless struggle, one which served no purpose save to increase their mutual hostility. For years on end Pirandello experienced daily the use of logical arguing and the impossibility of proving anything. In that totally disturbed relationship he knew fear, extreme alienation, and the spuriousness of his own arguments.

The insanity of his wife gave Pirandello the opportunity to study the psychosis created by an authoritarian society in its most extreme, most dramatic form. He himself wrote that a mad woman "led my hands as I wrote."

His mad wife was his inspiration. She showed him all the symptoms of a disturbance that he recognized in himself but had managed to conceal, being more robust than she. In his writings he identified himself with her, and expressed his own fears and aggressions. He saw through the cause of the disturbance. All the "mad" characters in his plays suffer their personality breakup under the pressure of an outside world that terrorized them, a world always cast in the mold of Sicilian society. Each is a victim of a scandal that led to exaggerated fears only because of the stagnant atmosphere of their atrophied society, fears that destroy the person and drive him forward in a despairing chase for ever new, ever more maniacal delusions.

2. Fascism

Pirandello found a general explanation for the feeling of insecurity, the insoluble contradiction between the living impulses of the individual and the demands made by society, in Bergsonian philosophy that at that time inspired the most varied world views and artistic styles—expressionism, surrealism, futurism, and jugendstil. (Jugendstil was the ornamental style that was current, especially for book decoration, at the turn of the century.) The Bergsonian concept of the contrast between "immutable form" and "fluid, continuously changing life" offered him an ideological formula for his own experience. To him this concept explained his diffuse inner opposition to the rigid conventionalism of life as a necessary flowing of the "feelings" (these, according to Bergson, were something "living, always changing and becoming") against the dominance of reason. In his 1908 essay on humor he wrote:

> Life is a continual flow that we try to bring to a standstill, to pinpoint, to seek in ourselves and outside. . . . Its forms . . . are the concepts, the ideals . . . all the fictions we create, the conditions, the situation, in which we try to find a firm footing. But within ourselves, in what we call our soul, and which is the life in us, the flow goes on, undefined, beneath the dams and outside the boundaries that we erect when we construct a conscience for ourselves and build up a personality. In certain stormy moments all our artificial constructs break miserably to pieces, inundated by the flood. But those elements that do not flow beneath the dams and beyond the boundaries but reveal themselves as something distinct from ourselves, that we have carefully canalized in our affections, in duties we have imposed on ourselves, in habits that we have established— these too burst their banks in certain moments of flood and turn everything upside down.

This, in the language of his philosophy, is a description of Pirandello's fundamental experience—the irrational suddenly breaking through the artificially stabilized security one has established. The revolutionary impulse, liberating what has been repressed, is granted justification by the concept of élan vital. It is seen as having the lawfulness of a natural force, as being an expression of universal life defying all human judgment. This concept of an anarchical life force, which became fundamental to Pirandello's thinking, paralleled the basic idea of Italian fascism, which drew its doctrine in part from the same philosophy.

At first Italian fascism was an irrational movement, inimical to history, imbued with antisocial and anti-institutional traits. The fascists wanted to destroy, to tear down a sick world, in which social discomfort and political indifference had been widespread for decades. More than other European states, the Italy of that period suffered from the consequences of the unsuccessful revolution of 1848. Risorgimento had indeed brought national unity and parliamentary government to Italy, but the expected changes in domestic and foreign policy had not taken place. Italy fell back into stagnation and was governed by a corrupt middle-class leadership, which was unable and unwilling to realize the grand concept of democratization.

Fascism was the last, and ultimately the most successful answer, to Italy's backwardness. But under fascism revolution became a mere emotionalism. Protests were made against the existing order, but no new plans were evolved. This revolutionary drive that comes to nothing was characteristic of Pirandello too.

Demands were made for social change, yet opposition to the old order of society remained on the level of angry outbursts and hysterical shouting.

The history of Italy since 1848 was for Pirandello the history of a corrupt and finally a lost utopia. His father had fought superbly during the Garibaldi street fighting; his mother had been the daughter of a Sicilian revolutionist expelled by the Bourbons. Sicily had been restless since 1848. It was the scene of frequent uprisings against the government that put them down with the help of the militia. While the child Luigi was listening to the heroic stories of the Garibaldi age told by his mother, he was experiencing simultaneously the ominous quiet and enforced silence of a country forcibly pacified—an example of revolution's impotence and reaction's violence.

But Pirandello's basic political disappointment came from the failure of the Sicilian socialist uprising in 1894. He himself had taken part in it, being then in his middle twenties. In 1892 he had openly declared himself for the radicals, had voted at the election for a candidate of the Fasci (the socialist party of Sicily), and had worked on the electoral committee. It is clear that he seriously believed in revolution. At any rate he wrote in a periodical in 1893 that "the sufferings of the people through a century had grown into a hurricane ready to shake up and overturn the old world." And he ended prophetically: "There can be no doubt that we are at the beginning of an important event. . . ."

This "important event" did not take place. The revolt of the Fasci, which had been directed against the economic exploitation of Sicily by the government, was suppressed by government groups. The movement faded out, and the country returned to its dubious status quo.

What this experience meant to Pirandello can be seen from the novel he wrote ten years later, *I vecchi e i giovani* (The Old and the Young). Here he used again the political events of the 1890s, now seen more clearly from a distance—the Sicilian uprising and the scandal of the Banca Romana, in which the government of that time was involved. Pirandello offered a picture of general corruption: the socialist uprising has wilted into a crude, aimless demonstration; the representatives of the Risorgimento are portrayed as grotesque or feeble creatures, rigid in their unassimilated ideals, unprincipled in their adaptation to the mediocre world around them. The point the novel makes is, as one of the characters expresses it, "to have understood the game . . . the game of that mocking little devil who lives in each one of us and amuses himself by showing us as an external reality what he immediately afterwards reveals to be our own illusion. . . . "

Pirandello seemed disillusioned. Events had made him skeptical, or rather, they had newly confirmed his original skepticism. But in the political disillusionment of the 1920s there remained a latent readiness to build utopias. He had lost his faith in revolution but not the feeling of dissatisfaction, the vague expectation of the occurrence of something new, of a radical transformation. It was this that later made him susceptible to fascism, despite all his doubts about political activity in general. When he joined the fascist party in 1924, he declared: "I am a fascist. And not only from today. I have been a fascist for thirty years. . . ."

His political commitments of 1894 and those of 1924 belonged together in his eyes despite the difference in essence and in goals that separated the movement of the Fasci from that of the fascists. What caught him was not so much the political intention as the power of an illusion to which he, lacking a critical world view of his own, fell prey. He joined in, whether as socialist or fascist, in perpetual flight from his own agnostic emptiness, in search of a means of salvation. He was susceptible to all the influences of the time, which he adapted to circumstances but which did not change his general attitude to life.

What drew him once more to politics when he allied himself with the fascists was, in addition to the desire for social change, a strong need for group identification, the emotion of patriotism, and, perhaps, opportunism. He was impressed by the fact that the fascists needed for their own ends the world reputation he had meanwhile acquired. Awed that Mussolini had invited him for a conversation, he did not hesitate to repay this interest by declaring unreserved loyalty to Mussolini. Thus he indicated unequivocal support for Mussolini's dictatorship. We hear nothing further of Pirandello's earlier doubts about its form, nothing further about his earlier inclination for anarchic opposition.

Like fascism itself, Pirandello had passed through an anarchist period to *normalizzazione*, the constructive phase of the movement. He wanted a policy of "action," of "reconstruction." For this reason, in order to "help fascism in its work of renewal and reconstruction," he joined the party. He did it at a time when the fascist regime was endangered by the assassination of Matteotti, in whose person Mussolini destroyed what remained of democracy. He was aware of the propaganda value of joining the party. In the interviews following his joining, Pirandello showed himself strongly antidemocratic, demanded the abolition of the freedom of the press, the abolition of parliament, and in general the speedy liquidation of everything "that was defunct and obstructive in the state." His reward from Mussolini was the subsidizing of a theater, the Teatro d'Arte, under Pirandello's directorship. Mussolini called it the *teatro del regime* (government theater) and was on hand for its opening in 1925.

Nevertheless, the alliance with fascism was ultimately a disappointment to Pirandello. In the new Italy his work was not to find the same response it had hitherto evoked. The atmosphere had changed. Pirandellism went out of fashion. His own new works lacked the immediacy of experience. In the main they repeated the old themes, with greater technical proficiency. Finally, even he came to see how his last play, *The Mountain Giants*, betrayed the fact that the dictatorship hampered artistic development and destroyed the aesthetic sensibilities of the public. Mussolini continued to turn to him in theatrical matters, and asked him for plans for a national theater in 1926. But Pirandello's ideas were never realized. His own theater fared worse and worse. He himself had to tour with his company, but that too came to an end in 1928 for lack of subsidies.

Pirandello came to feel more and more isolated. He found that blind accommodation to the authorities not only was not preserving him from nihilistic despair but was only leading to deeper inner isolation. Externally he continued to adapt himself, though often, it is true, in an ambiguous way. In 1929 he accepted membership in the newly founded Accademia d'Italia, let them put him into a parade uniform with a two-peaked cap, and began his speech with homage to Mussolini. But in the same speech he also publicly attacked Gabriele D'Annunzio, the zealous party member and declared friend of the regime. He very nearly created a scandal. But toward the end of the speech he showed himself once again to be pro-fascist by criticizing Giovanni Verga (whose work he had earlier praised out of conviction) for his pessimistic outlook in contradistinction to the optimism of the government.

This looks like cynicism. In fact it is merely a reaction of uncertainty and fear in a paradoxical, incurably divided world. Adaptation was for Pirandello an act of legitimate self-defense. In his essay on humor he wrote:

> The necessity for mutual deception is directly proportionate to the difficulty of the struggle for survival and to the person's awareness of his own weakness in this struggle. The pretense of strength, honor, sympathy, intelligence, in short of every virtue including the greatest, honesty, is a form of adaptation, a handy weapon in the struggle.

That it is necessary for man to deliberately project an image of adaptation to others while concealing rebellion, that survival demands that one do this, is the lesson Pirandello gleaned from an unstable social environment. It was this lesson that led him to fascism. His attitude toward fascism was only a repetition of the attitude that he had always seen as the only possible one: "Each one must arrange his mask as best he can—his outer mask. For inside of it there is the inner mask, which often fails to square with the outer. And nothing is true!"

Fascism was not able to alter this view. His last years were filled with bitter resignation and restlessness. His state of mind, he wrote in 1931 to his daughter, was "without peace and without any kind of hope. I no longer have a home, a country of my own. My mind is completely alienated. I can no longer make contact with anything or anyone." That is the other, the inner mask of Pirandello, the mask that remained his despite all the external adjustments that he felt required to make. It reveals the melancholy of an aimless soul deprived of every tie.

3. Sicilian Dialect Theater and the Theater of the Grotesque

Pirandello's emergence as a dramatist began abruptly. It was sparked off by outside forces. In the course of tidying the books in the Pirandello apartment in 1916, a friend discovered an old manuscript of a play by Pirandello. He sent it to one of his friends, Nino Martoglio, who was in charge of a Sicilian theatrical company. Martoglio was enchanted by the play. With his principal actor, Angelo Musco, who badly needed a new part, Martoglio begged Pirandello for a play for the Sicilian dialect theater. At first Pirandello refused. But when Martoglio persisted, he finally helped him to sketch out a play that the company put on in Milan. Unexpectedly successful, it earned a good deal of money.

This probably encouraged Pirandello, who was not earning much as a teacher in a girl's college, to make his own independent attempt. In the same year, 1916, he wrote for Martoglio's company the comedy, *Think, Giacomino!*, which was performed in Rome in July. It won so much acclaim that Pirandello followed it immediately with two other plays in the local dialect, *Cap and Bells* and *Liolà*, which were equally successful. From that moment on the theater held him in its grip. With a productivity that verged on the demonic he wrote twenty-eight plays in the succeeding eight years —among them was *Six Characters in Search of an Author*, which made him world famous. This writing earned him the Nobel Prize in 1934.

In 1916 Pirandello was almost fifty years old. He had written short novels, essays, and five full-length novels, one of which, *Il fu Mattia Pascal* (1904; The Late Mattia Pascal), had made him known in Italy and abroad. He was content with his success and saw himself exclusively as a narrative writer. For years he used to say that the theater did not interest him. He had even developed a theory about drama being a second-rate art form, only the imitation of an original work of art that loses its essential character, its substance, through being transposed onto the stage. When his friends, many of whom were critics or playwrights, spoke about the theater, he made a show of indifference, fell silent, and laid out the cards for solitaire, while they carried on a voluble discussion.

Pirandello's dislike of the theater had something forced and artificial about it. It concealed a secret disappointment. In fact, the theater had delighted him in childhood, stimulating him to his first literary efforts. While a student in Palermo (1886) and later in Rome (1887–89) he had written various plays, which, according to the accounts he gave of them to his sister, already revealed typically Pirandellian themes and an original dramatic talent.

One of these plays, *Birds That Fly High*, required effects that turned the orchestra into a stage and the audience into players, in the manner of a Greek chorus. The birds that fly high were crazy birds, tossed by storms and tempests, flying ever further afield, without knowing where, whereas the hens and cocks, the town birds, scratched about in the dirt, and laughed at the birds that passed over their heads, screeching as if they were cursing. Another play was called *The Rehearsal: Dramatic Scenes*.

Thus Pirandello's later work for the theater clearly had its beginnings in his youth. But his experiences with the world of the theater were so discouraging that he switched to narrative writing, suppressing the wish to write for the stage, and destroyed his first dramatic efforts, for which he was unable to find a theater.

In the 1890s he once again tried to make a beginning with a play called *Epilogue* (later published as *The Vise*, 1908). It was, however, given to an actor who had so many reservations about it that Pirandello wrote him a furious letter. The answer was a challenge to a duel, which was only withdrawn through the intervention of friends. The episode left Pirandello with a powerful dislike of everything that had to do with the theater. He continued to write plays, especially one-act plays, but he did nothing about them. Even when *The Vise* and *Sicilian Limes* were eventually produced in 1910, he was still constricted by the psychological block he had in the meantime developed about the theater.

His liberation from such inhibition was accomplished only by the success of *Think, Giacomino!* and by the simultaneous emergence of a "new theater" in Italy, the theater of the grotesque. In the same year that *Think, Giacomino!* was premiered, a theater in Rome offered Luigi Chiarelli's grotesque play, *The Mask and the Face.* This was the harbinger of a wave of grotesque plays on the Italian stage. Up to the beginning of the 1920s a number of Italian playwrights—Luigi Chiarelli, Luigi Antonelli, Rosso di San Secondo, Enrico Cavacchioli, and others—regularly supplied the theater with plays that were highly fanciful parodies of the old bourgeois sentimental theater. Chiarelli later described the state of the Italian theater of 1914 in these words:

> At that time it was impossible to go to the theater without encountering languishing, talkative descendants of Marguerite Gautier or Rose Bernd, or lazy camp followers of Oswald or Cyrano. The public shed sentimental tears and left the theater depressed. But the next evening

it met again in large numbers to applaud a spicy little sketch such as *Le pillole d'Ercole*, in order to restore its moral and social balance.

The theater of the grotesque saw itself as a protest against the naturalistic drama of Ibsen and Gerhart Hauptmann, and the pseudoromantic drama of Alexandre Dumas *fils*. It wanted to stir up a public that gave itself unthinkingly and uncritically to any and every influence. The theater of the grotesque exaggerated the tearful bourgeois tragedies, and turned them into hair-raising melodramas or into farce. It harked back to an old Italian tradition—the commedia dell'arte, in which incredible and fantastic situations were created for Arlecchino, Pulcinella, and Pantalone, in order to keep the audience in a perpetual state of astonishment. In the theater of the grotesque that now monopolized the stage, coincidence was heaped upon coincidence. In much the same way, the action became arbitrarily mechanical, the characters lost their individualities and were turned into puppets. The old bourgeois theater still provided the plot, which, however, had become so twisted and devoid of meaning that the tragic seemed comic, and the comic tragic.

This style of drama well suited Pirandello's own dramatic gifts. He looked on it as "a farce which in presenting a tragedy included its self-parody and self-caricature, but not as superimposed elements; instead they were like the projections of shadows from its own body, awkward shadows that accompanied every tragic gesture." This was the way he described his own work in his essay on humor. He saw himself as a humorist who is suspended between laughter and tears, a humorist who cannot give himself to an emotion without perceiving something that makes faces at him that fill him with anxiety, bewilderment and rage.

This mixture of the tragic and the comic was for him the mark of every true work of humor. He traced its historical ancestry back to romantic irony and German idealism. He referred to the modern Italian theater of the grotesque as transcendental farce and explained this with reference to Hegelian philosophy, according to which the "I, the only true reality, can smile at the empty show of the universe. For what the universe builds up it can as easily pull down: it cannot take its own creations seriously."

Here Pirandello was referring above all to the romantic and idealistic roots of his own plays. The fact that he rediscovered these in the theater of the grotesque confirmed his views and encouraged him in ideas that he himself found "very bold" and would earlier not have dared to introduce on the stage. But at the same time he remained independent of the theater of the grotesque. From the beginning, he was preoccupied with his own personal themes and his own unmistakable style. Whereas other writers of grotesque plays were unable to free themselves from traditional theatrical forms, being only able to squander their talent in pursuit of ever more fanciful and increasingly abstract performances, Pirandello added his own original dramatic ideas to the traditional forms.

For decades he had, at first under the influence of Giovanni Verga and of verismo, and then increasingly in independence of verismo, offered in his fiction his very own subject matter—role-playing and the break-up of the personality, in a disturbed, mechanized world. His characters were puppets, but puppets passionately provoked and provoking, actors knowing they were acting, automatons possessing enigmatic, complex psychologies. They talked and thought aloud in concise and rapid words whose pent-up energy had an immediate dramatic effect on the audience.

Pirandello had already revealed himself as a dramatist in his novels. Many of these can now be seen as dramatic sketches. Now that a theater was accessible to him he often adapted these sketches for the stage. Often it was a matter of a few days' work because he was able to transfer whole passages of dialogue unchanged into the new medium.

At the same time he developed, more consistently than did the other writers of the theater of the grotesque, a critical attitude toward the theater. He remained suspicious, reserved, basically hostile. What he was engaged in was disguised antitheater, the infiltration of theatrical conventions by surprise effects that distorted the roles played by individuals and groups, and lengthened, shortened, and finally shattered the construction of the play. He let the husband appear as procurer, the outsider as solid citizen, the governess as prostitute. He delayed the action by reflections, snatched it up for a punchline, repeated the story at several different levels so as to have the versions annul and reflect each other, interchanged theater and reality, actors and public. And at the end the audience was left without solution or program, irritated and bewildered by the jumble of contradictions that the old, tidy, easily comprehensible theater of illusion had become.

Pirandello made use of all the approaches developed by the contemporary theater in its efforts to free itself from the theater of the nineteenth century. He was open to the most diverse influences: to the romantic theater, above all Ludwig Tieck, who had anticipated the play within the play, the interchange of audience and actors, and the arbitrariness of construction in *Puss in Boots* and *Upside-Down World*; to the commedia dell'arte, from which he derived the faster pace of his performances, the short effective scenes, the character types, the gags, and the jumbled-up exaggerations of the action; to the modern Russian theater, which fascinated him with the mobility of its stage effects and its emphasis on the dramatic.

But all improvisation and experimentation, all comic situations and innovations, were measured by him against the trauma in his mind. The stage was for him the projection of an alienation that he repeated and on which he reflected. Into the clichés of domestic dramas and dramas of jealousy, which he coarsened into puppet shows, he inserted awareness, reflection. His characters think, argue, theorize, try by all rational means to resolve their emotional problems. Pirandello considered the introduction of this intellectual element as his true achievement in the theater.

He felt that one of the innovations he introduced was the transformation of "intellect into emotion." This transformation was not always successful. In the forty or more plays he wrote, he sometimes slid into abstraction or sentimentality. His ideology, whose validity he accepted uncritically, often blinded his intellect and made his passion into a superfluous demonstration. But in his best plays, he succeeded in raising the drama to a new dimension without sacrificing the immediacy of the performance or its dramatic substance. He also succeeded in deepening the plays and freeing them from traditional concepts.

Here one can learn from Pirandello. T. S. Eliot said of Pirandello that all serious dramatists of his generation and the next were in Pirandello's debt, that he had pointed out the direction that contemporary dramatists could turn to in the search for solutions.

4. The Plays on the Stage

Pirandello's plays won unusually quick acclaim in the early 1920s. They were received with an almost hysterical enthusiasm. After the production of *Six Characters in Search of an Author* in Rome in 1921, the Pirandello fashion spread like wildfire to almost all the countries of the world. The fever even reached the provinces; and audiences, critics, producers and actors alike, were thrown into a very frenzy of passion for the theater.

Between 1922 and 1925, *Six Characters*, translated into twenty-five languages, staged by the most famous producers, played one hundred and thirty-one times in the Reinhardt theater alone and became one of the most frequently produced and discussed plays in the world. Other plays followed.

In Germany twelve Pirandello plays were produced within three years, in France fourteen plays were performed in Pirandello's lifetime, and in New York City one theater devoted an entire season to Pirandello. Pirandello dominated the stage, and even though the critics at times protested, audiences remained enthusiastic.

Six Characters in particular seems to have caught the mood of postwar audiences. The stimulating idea, the fluid action, scintillating and ironic, and the ecstasy of a deep, not altogether fathomable emotionalism, found an echo in the unstable atmosphere of the 1920s, when people were constantly seeking innovations. Pirandello provided them with sensation, and producers regarded the stage as a field for experimenting, vying with each other in surpassing the dramatists in surprise effects.

Twilight in their hands became still dimmer, magic still more magical, the dramatic still more dramatic. Pirandello's plays served as displays for the brilliant artistry of producers such as Max Reinhardt or Georges Pitoëff, and critics praised the "creativity" of the producers more highly than they praised the plays.

"Once again," wrote Monty Jacobs after Reinhardt's production of *Six Characters*, "the spectator warms his heart at the richness of Reinhardt's imaginative power, and feasts his senses on the lights and colors of his theatrical genius." And in Paris Pitoëff turned the play into a sensational success by lowering the characters onto the stage or a moving platform, against a mysteriously illuminated green background.

When Pirandello himself traveled with his company through Europe and America in 1925 and brought with him his own plays, it became clear that he saw them differently—in his hands they were clearer, more real, and more vehement. People were astonished, somewhat disenchanted, and even slightly annoyed by this Italian theater that "handled so adroitly," as Julius Meyer-Graefe wrote, "the northern intellectual art [drama]." Meyer-Graefe sensed something "hostile to Reinhardt" in Pirandello's production, an inclination to "play off native ideas against foreign customs." And he insisted that *Six Characters*, a play that was a "typical product of modern Europe," could only be produced with German methods.

But the Italian production accorded with Pirandello's intentions. He had formed his company by hard training into an organ that implemented his own conception of his plays. Pirandello shunned scenic extravagance, allure, display. His aim was always to bring the play to life from within, to obtain his effects not by means of elaborate staging but from his own direct experience, which he wanted to transfer onto the stage in the most direct way possible. He told the actors to penetrate into the character they were playing, to enter into that character as into a diving suit. They were to identify with the character. This was still the naturalistic school, the Stanislavsky method.

In imitation of Stanislavsky, Pirandello went through the different parts with his actors before every rehearsal, analyzing them or showing the actors how they should be played. He himself was a natural actor. When he read the text aloud he changed with startling rapidity and intensity into the different characters. One observer reported:

> His face is of an incredible mobility. In fact it makes one think of a number of faces. He repeats

and copies the distortions of the actors' faces. . . .
The mouth that runs through the gamut of all its
possible expressions, turns into innumerable
mouths, the chin trembles convulsively, the
nerves are tensed to breaking point, the face is
full of lightning expressions. . . . The scene develops, works to a climax . . . between two,
three, four characters, and Pirandello turns into
these two, three, four characters. He keeps pace
with the crescendo by multiplying his expressions; accentuates it with his whole bearing . . .
with the tormented movement of his whole person. He mutters the angry words with unheard-
of force, his chin sunk on his breast, and his teeth
gnashing. . . . Silent and more effective than all
the rest.

His performance had a magical, almost demonic
effect on the actors. They were fascinated, and his
mood transferred itself to them. His best actors, in
particular Marta Abba and Lamberto Picasso, developed a similar directness, a similarly passionate tempo
and temperament, and an astonishing capacity for
transformation. The whole company played in the
same breathlessly expressive Pirandellian rhythm.

Maintaining this extremely fast, overheated pace,
that was only broken by a few silent moments, Pirandello achieved a state of explosiveness that, despite
its depths and psychology, had elements of parody
in it. The tension directed entirely outward was also
distortion. The tragedy—as Pirandello, the humorist,
demanded—turned into farce that included within it
"parody and caricature as broad shadows of every
tragic gesture." Here the production went beyond

pure naturalism. It transcended it with its own methods, overemphasized the natural until it became "unnatural" and grotesque.

So that this leaping from the tragic into the comic should not become mannered but should appear on the stage with all the freshness and flexibility of the present moment, Pirandello had each play performed after five to six days' rehearsal, banished the prompter, and rehearsed the actors, in the manner of the commedia dell'arte, in the improvisation of a theme. By this means he obtained a performance of comic originality that came closest to his own conception of art as the creation of a sudden idea.

Of modern producers it was Eric Bentley above all who adhered to the tragic and grotesque elements intended by Pirandello himself in the performance of his plays. Others have tried to reinterpret Pirandello with emphasis on the intellect, individual psychology, or the imagination. They have put the characters in different dresses, supplemented the play with explanatory writings by Pirandello, or added new scenes. The open-endedness of Pirandello's plays permits this but does not require it. Their effectiveness and actuality are as much a part of them as the indestructible fascination that derives from the play and interplay of the characters.

More than with other writers, however, ever new interpretations of Pirandello lead to new insights. The complex structure of his play points in many different directions—to Grand Guignol as to psychology, to poetic realism as to the theater of the absurd. In between lie all kinds of gradations as they result from different combinations and contrasts. To discover these remains a constant stimulus and challenge in the theater. Perhaps this will lead to the long-awaited but still delayed Pirandellian renascence.

The discussion of the stage productions of the dramas analyzed in *Plays* is provided in the individual chapters.

PLAYS

Cap and Bells

CONTENTS: The scene is a small town in the center of Sicily, in the provincial but ornate drawing room of the Fioricas. Beatrice Fiorica suspects her husband of deceiving her with the wife of Ciampa, an employee in his office. Just the suspicion is very disturbing to her. She makes up her mind to catch the lovers red-handed. While her husband is traveling, she baits the trap. She sends Ciampa to Palermo, so that he will not get in the way. She then informs the police, who hide one of their men in Ciampa's apartment. Signor Fiorica is thereupon caught with the wife of Ciampa. There is a scandal, but there is no actual proof of adultery. People are angry for a time, but then the whole thing blows over. Ciampa, however, threatens to turn the episode into a tragedy. He feels himself humiliated, finds the slander intolerable, and vows to kill his wife and Fiorica with an ax. Fifi, Beatrice's brother, saves the situation by explaining that the gossip was simply an idèe fixe of Beatrice's.

This gives Ciampa the idea that she should pretend to be mad and enter an institution temporarily. "Then I am disarmed, and I will need no further satisfaction." Beatrice at first refuses to fall in with Ciampa's request, but she finally acquiesces. She imitates his cocklike crowing. She is led off while he breaks out into terrible laughter.

Cap and Bells, the third of the dialect plays with which Pirandello made his debut on the Sicilian stage, is the first of his plays to demonstrate the full complexity of his work.

The ideas contained in his earlier play, *Professor Toti*, were already truly Pirandellian in conception. The comedy of the seventy-year-old schoolteacher who marries the pregnant sixteen-year-old daughter of his beadle for love of her and the child, and forces her young lover into a *marriage à trois*, turns life upside down and attacks bourgeois morality. The play, nevertheless, is a comedy in the traditional style, in which the structure remains intact, the protagonist inviolable. In *Cap and Bells*, on the other hand, there is a new element. Ciampa, the hero, is vulnerable. He is inwardly hurt, loses his equilibrium, and has to make great efforts to try to recover it. Thus the theatrical conflict becomes an inner one: it moves into that dark sphere where powerful emotions are engendered, which express themselves in shrill outcries, which bring disorder into the plot, and which, after the second act, break off with a lightninglike turn.

The story that underlies *Cap and Bells* is of no special power. It is one of the usual stories of adultery and takes a relatively undramatic course. But through the characterization of Ciampa the play becomes exciting and through Ciampa, an eccentric character, Pirandello projects for the first time the full extent of the conflict that creates the distortion of the individual by the social pattern. Ciampa has adapted himself, but he is one of those whose adaptation conceals wounds that make his reactions unpredictable and dangerous. He himself speaks of those wounds only toward the end of the play, and then only in quite general terms.

Ciampa asks Beatrice,

> "Can you imagine why a man commits murder? Or why a poor old, maybe ugly, fellow—for love of his wife who grips his heart tight as in a vise, who stops every cry of pain with a kiss under which he swoons away intoxicated—can you imagine, signora, what humiliations this old fellow expects, even to the extent of sharing the love of his wife with another man, a young, rich, and handsome man, so long as she lets him believe that he is master in his house and so long as no one notices what is happening? I speak in general terms, you understand. I do not speak of myself. Those are wounds, signora, wounds that one hides in shame."

We must not make this psychological motive, which Ciampa admits while also denying it, into the key to the whole play. It is as little the total truth as anything else that comes to the surface in *Cap and Bells* or any other Pirandello play. It is simply the reverse side of the façade that Ciampa untiringly displays to society. But in this stereotype of the cuckold, made cowardly because of his enslavement, there is an underlying element of disquiet and irrationality. His life energy is blocked because it cannot express itself in the role society has assigned to Ciampa.

Ciampa thus becomes a perfect example of society itself, with one difference: that he is aware of the tension and foresees its ultimate consequences. He is aware of the volcanic subsoil on which society rests. That is why he can illustrate the drama of society in his own person. He personifies the vicious circle in which society continually represses those elements of life that threaten its order, constantly increasing their potential explosiveness. Thus the conflict tightens, becoming denser instead of resolving itself. On the surface it becomes smaller, more reified, while it is becoming more internalized, and more conscious.

The play develops out of this mounting tension that expresses itself on a stage that is in transition from traditional marriage drama to drama of the grotesque. The scenes in which Ciampa does not appear are conventional theater, featuring jealousy and intrigue. They are like the old-style drawing-room comedy that does not continue with the confronting of material it cannot handle. The theatrical shorthand lies like a mask, cipherlike, over the inflammable matter of an uncontrolled excitement. The scenes are so conventionally theatrical that their very conventionality attracts attention.

Beatrice is the embodiment of a jealous woman, whose character is reduced to the single motive of revenge. She focuses on her obsession with a frenzied rage from which nothing can distract her. When the curtain rises, she can be seen sitting on a divan, crying; she is "pale, hysterical, often balancing between excitement and depression." Her behavior is reflected in the cruder, less interesting behavior of the Saracen woman, an old peddler and paid snooper, who confirms Beatrice's suspicions and inflames her jealousy. In this figure of the typical intriguer, as in the other subordinate characters—Fana, the old servant; Fifi, an elegant young man; Spano, the assistant police commissioner—Pirandello is creating stock characters that seem to be derived from characters in traditional Italian popular comedy. They have few individual characteristics. Their talk and behavior are stylized, thus reflecting the typical patterns of social behavior. Pirandello uses them as catalysts in the unfolding of the action. They are made to represent society, a society that allows dangerous energies to surface without knowing what it is doing.

Thus the Saracen woman, by her gossip, inflames Beatrice's rage to the point where she decides to teach her husband a lesson. And Fifi, a typical man about town, who attempts to smooth over the whole affair with a flow of words, only succeeds in hastening the climax. The police inspector who tries to get at the truth, in the opposite way, by using his official authority brings about the same result.

It is typical of Pirandello's dramatic technique that he sets against these stereotypes of the traditional theater, to whom he grants their simple identity and relative naturalness, one or more other figures who have lost awareness of their own identity and therefore quite clearly show themselves to be masks. The conventional social pattern, which upholds the former characters with rigid naiveté, breaks down. Through the mask-wearing characters it betrays its defects, not in order to make room for a new utopian pattern but to refashion itself more insistently, more despairingly than ever. Ciampa is the first Pirandellian dramatic characterization to demonstrate in his own person this process of self-construction, which, according to Pirandello, is the basis of his art. But it always shows itself to be a false construction, a reification of the customary roles.

Ciampa's appearance is wholly disguise. He has "thick, long, untidy hair combed back, and mutton-chop whiskers. His eyes flash, hard and piercing, behind his strong spectacles. A penholder sticks out from behind his right ear. He wears an old, slightly too tight jacket." This is a mask that no longer fits. Behind it a contradictory mask appears. The mutton-chop whiskers juxtaposed to the untidy hair, the glasses in front of the hard, piercing eyes, the old too-tight jacket—all these exaggerate the failure of the attempt he has made, one he was compelled to make, to adapt to the bourgeois pattern. In the end Ciampa remains only a caricature of a man who, with pen behind ear, comically emphasizes his social position. Even his behavior is stagey—an effective, continuously improved construction. His thoughts break out of him in disconnected phrases, metaphors and similes. He is submissive and excitable by turns. His words point to something unformulated, to fear and aggression. He is overtouchy, overhasty, forever anticipating suspicion in others. Without being asked he insists on the respectability of his wife, his own indispensability in the office. He is forever secretly warning and questioning.

But when he hears that he is to go to Palermo, he springs suddenly, ecstatically, to the opposite extreme:

"I come alive, dear Signor Fifi, when I can breathe the air of a large town, like Palermo. I am stifling here, Signora! This is no life for me! But the moment my feet are on the pavements of a large town, I feel as though I am no longer earthbound. I feel as though I'm in paradise. Ideas simply come to me. The blood rushes in my veins. Oh—if only I had been born there, or in any other town on the mainland—who knows what I might have become!"

This too is histrionic exaggeration—a mask. But it is one that casts doubt on the mask of the timid provincial.

For a brief moment Ciampa's suppressed energies have burst out. He has the illusion of boundless possibilities opening out, possibilities that reach beyond his oppressive small-town Sicilian life. But he admits this feeling only to suppress it all the more violently. "We must not exaggerate. We are puppets, dear Signor Fifi! The divine spirit enters into us, and the next moment he is a puppet. You, I—we are all puppets." And every puppet wants to be respected. "Not so much as the person he considers himself to be, but in the role he assumes outside."

Here Pirandello develops the argument to the point where Ciampa's particular case turns into the general human situation, and where something of the ideological assumptions of the play become apparent, even though only in cliché form. Ciampa no longer explains

himself in the naturalistic manner as a victim of cir-
cumstance. Now he explains himself as a victim of a
metaphysical necessity that affects all men. His desperate drive to give his life a definite shape and form
is the expression of an inherent consequence, as
Pirandello explained it. This desire is the contrary
tendency to a complete annihilation of the life force
that works in him. "Life," according to Pirandello, "is
a devastating river that plunges into dizzying, white
flat plains of infinite expanse. Woe to us if we glance
into that primordial life. We become rigid and at the
same time we become godheads. We cease being
human, and our contact with average people becomes
impossible."

Ciampa is one of those who have caught a glimpse
of "primordial life." He is marked, "ceases to be
human," his contact with the average person is broken.
Behind the social mask laboriously held up in front
lies concealed the specter of a "life" hardened to
monstrous proportions. When he reappears on the
stage after the scandal has erupted, the garb of the
good citizen has fallen away. "He is pale as a corpse,
dirty, his forehead is bleeding, his collar undone, the
tie hanging loose, his spectacles in his hand." His
appearance is overexcited, almost farcical. His increasingly theatrical and violent behavior alarms those who
have rushed in vain to try to calm him: Fifi, Spano,
Fana, Beatrice's mother, and Beatrice herself. He
tramples on his hat, tears open his jacket: "See the
heart . . . the bleeding heart of a man who has been
wounded to death." He breaks out in sobs and suddenly holds out his arms toward Spano: "Feel my
pulse. Tell me if it is beating faster. I tell you here,

quite calmly, you and all of you are witnesses, that this evening or tomorrow, as soon as she gets home, I will kill my wife with an ax. And not only her—that would probably be a favor only to the signora. I shall kill Signor Fiorica as well."

Thus Pirandello brings the conflict to a visible climax, then creates the following axiom: the more extreme the unmasking, the more powerful the drive to stereotype oneself, to turn oneself into a puppet. The compulsion to play a social role degenerates into brutality. Killing for honor remains for Ciampa a way held open to him, the deceived husband, by Sicilian society. Ciampa's reaction appears to be staged. It remains a play within the play. But that too makes for terror. Panic leaps over to the bystanders, who push it away from themselves and project the madness onto Beatrice, the guilty one.

Fifi impresses upon Ciampa: "The whole scandal was only brought about by an idée fixe." All agree with him and confirm what he said: "An idée fixe, Ciampa. An idée fixe." Ciampa accepts this as the explanation. He orders Beatrice to pack her things: "Everybody has recognized this: and that is why you are mad! You are mad, and therefore you must go into a madhouse."

The tension that can no longer be dealt with psychologically is resolved by a Pirandellian trick that expresses the idea of the play in the most direct way possible. Pirandello had Beatrice, improbably enough, give way. She submits "as though under a compulsion." She constructs her own role, plays the part of a madwoman. The anarchic forces she has released suddenly crystallize into craziness. Nothing is changed.

As Ciampa says, everything is "calmly and peacefully put right." Only protest remains. The final scene goes back to the beginning. Urged by Ciampa, Beatrice as though possessed, breaks out in a loud cock-a-doodle-doo. She continues to cry out the truth in people's faces—that Ciampa is a cuckold. But the truth is now only a parody of itself. It is the impotent fool's license, proof of a madness that can be safely confined within the walls of an asylum.

The disturbance that has briefly laid bare the sub-soil that underlies life in an idyllic small town is once more covered over, this time more deliberately and hopelessly. The end is laughter, "a terrible laughter, of rage, despair, and wild joy," which is Ciampa's ultimate comment. This cuts off the dialogue. The play becomes a meaningless, inarticulate protest against an absurd world.

Dramatic vision seems to have shrunk here in favor of the ideas that not only inflate the play but also run ahead of it with their unspoken assumptions. What is actually shown does not quite include everything that is meant to be proved. The action moves forward, shaping the play into a calculated, almost parablelike construct, an abstract movement that brings it to a finish with a deliberate gag.

But all this is fleshed out and supported by the dramatic vitality of Ciampa. He fulfills Pirandello's requirements for the theater in being a "person who makes drama." By his manipulative power he turns all the ideas and stratagems, the sudden transitions and violence of the play, into a living reality, as immediate as it is fantastic.

Thus It Is (If It Seems So to You)

CONTENTS: In the parlor of provincial councilor Agazzi, people are discussing the "case" of a family of three that has recently moved to this town after their own village had been destroyed by an earthquake. The behavior of the family is puzzling. They make no visits, live only by themselves. But they do not live together. Signor Ponza, secretary at the prefecture, and his wife, who never shows herself in public, have taken up residence in a suburban apartment. Ponza's mother-in-law, Signora Frola, has settled in the center of the town. Signora Frola, for some reason, cannot live with her daughter or even visit her in her apartment. Two or three times a day she can be seen standing in the courtyard of the Ponza apartment, calling up to her daughter. The daughter then appears on the balcony and sends letters down to the old woman in a little basket that hangs by a long rope from the railings.

The inhabitants of this small Italian town would like

to know what lies behind all this. One after another they summon Signora Frola, Signor Ponza, and finally Signora Ponza, and subject them to an interrogation. But each time the story becomes more incomprehensible, crazier, and even more mysterious. Signora Frola explains, by way of excuse, that her son-in-law loves his wife with such passion that he permits no one, not even his wife's own mother, to penetrate this world of "love." Signor Ponza declares his mother-in-law to be crazy. His wife, he says, is not her daughter at all; she is his second wife. His first wife, Signora Frola's daughter, had died four years ago. Finally Signora Ponza herself throws light on this maze of contradictions. At the prefect's request she is brought into the Agazzi house and there reveals one truth. She is both Signora Frola's daughter and the second wife of Signor Ponza. But for herself she is no one. For others she is "whoever they take her to be."

With *Thus It Is*, Pirandello successfully makes the leap from dialect theater to national theater. The play was very successfully performed in Milan in 1917 and still continues to be one of his most frequently staged plays. With this play Pirandello knew that he had written something exceptional. "It is . . . really more a parable than a comedy," he wrote to his son. "I am pleased with it. It certainly is of striking originality. But I do not know whether I can place it, because of the unusual boldness of the situation. . . . Friends say it is the best thing I have so far done. I think so too. . . ."

By the critics the play was greatly praised and violently condemned in equal proportions. Benedetto

Croce, who in any case did not care for Pirandello's "hermeneutic sophistries," held that the play confirmed his own judgment that Pirandello's dramatic style consisted of a "few artistic" strokes "that are then overlaid and distorted by a cramped and illogical philosophizing." The "steadfastness of ironic compassion could have been the artistic core of the play," he said rebukingly, "if the author had not preferred to turn his play into a parable to illustrate the thesis that 'truth is what you think it is.' "

These criticisms are in part justified, but they overlook the example Pirandello used to present his thesis that seemingly deals only with the theory of cognition. The new and interesting element in the play is not its parabolic nature, the way in which it illustrates an abstract philosophy, but its innovative transformation of drawing-room comedy into social satire. What Pirandello demonstrates with the devices of elegant drawing-room comedy is his development of the problematical character of society.

The "truth" that is sought concerns a mysterious social situation that gives rise in the townspeople to anxiety: the threat of anarchy. In the curious behavior of the Frola-Ponza family, society suspects something that conflicts with its coercive system, a dumb, challenging world of its own that surreptitiously undermines the conventional pattern. Summoning together all the terror of public opinion and the small-town apparatus of law and order—the prefect, the commissioner—the townspeople try to solve the mysterious situation, to render it again socially acceptable.

But the hearing to which they summon the family meets with irrational resistance. Before the judgment seat of society, the accused turn into puppets, and their answers to pure constructs hide the unspoken truth. In a crazy way they act "theater" that answers society's questions about the truth with ever new roles, new clichés—in an ever madder exchange of masks.

The story begins with councilor Agazzi's complaint to the prefect that Ponza, the secretary of the prefecture, refused to allow his wife to receive Agazzi's wife and daughter when they came to visit Signora Ponza. At a nod from above, the whole thing starts moving. Signora Frola, a "slight, modestly but neatly dressed, old woman," whose sadness is "tempered by a gentle smile," appears at the Agazzi apartment and makes her apologies. Out of this grows a manic situation.

The company—Signor and Signora Agazzi, their daughter, Signor and Signora Sirelli, and Signora Cini —rush toward Signora Frola. Lusting with curiosity, they ask ever more obtrusive questions, relentlessly penetrating into the unknown and appropriating it.

An equally compulsive counter urge to conceal what is her intimate secret grows in Signora Frola. Step by step they draw from her an explanation that, on closer examination, is shown to be false. Her explanations about the terrible earthquake that has destroyed her village and killed its inhabitants only arouses further questions.

After such a misfortune, says Signora Sirelli, feeling her way, the survivors must surely feel the need to stay together? But Signora Frola counters this with another cliché. She thinks children should be left to themselves after they are married. But Signora Cini presses further. Surely Signora Ponza often comes to visit her mother and keep her company? This has its effect on Signora Frola. She becomes confused. The others at once press their advantage. The conversation becomes quick, excited, sharpens into a cross-examination. Signora Frola, dismayed, says one thing after another until she gives up, seemingly exhausted. "Well then. I probably must tell you. It is a feeling, a feeling, signore, that is very hard to understand." Her son-in-law wants to have his wife all to himself. He has locked up his wife in a world of love in which she "must live without ever stepping out of it and into which no one person must ever be allowed to enter." It is enough for her to know her daughter is happy. "And now," she says, "in the course of time, I have, if I may say so, reconciled myself to it." In this way she stressed the hypothetical character of her explanation.

The company has what it needs—an "explanation" —but Signor Ponza appears unexpectedly. His very appearance is enough to confirm their expectation of a monster. He is a "squat, threatening-looking man, with thick black hair, low forehead, and a big black moustache. . . . He wears a black suit, his eyes are unflickeringly fixed, gloomy." Excitement seems to be getting the better of him. "Tense, with clenched fists, exhibiting suppressed violence, he wipes the sweat from his brow with a black-bordered handkerchief."

Now he proceeds to give his explanation. "Signora Frola is mad." She thinks he does not want to let her see her daughter. But her daughter is dead, and she obstinately insists that his second wife is her daughter. Out of pity they let her persist in her illusion, but he cannot expect his wife to live with a stranger and to accept a stranger's caresses. He feels he should explain this. Because he is a public official, he cannot have people saying that out of jealousy or some other reason he prevents a mother from seeing her own daughter.

But as soon as Signor Ponza has gone and the gathering is trying to adjust itself to this new situation, Signora Frola appears again and leads them to complete amazement with the real truth. Her son-in-law is not mad, no, but he is obsessed by an idée fixe. He believes that his first wife, her daughter, is dead. But in fact she had only been taken to a sanatarium to protect her from his frenzied love. Since then he no longer recognizes her. To calm him, they had to fake a second marriage. Her daughter now has to pretend that she is someone else. And she, the mother, has to pretend that she herself is mad.

The situation is not devoid of comedy. The jack-in-the-box-like to-ing and fro-ing of persons and explanations, the pathos and redundancy of talk, the grotesque theatricality of Signor Ponza and the sugary sentimentality of Signora Frola, seem like parodies of a real situation. In spite of this there remain factual shock and wild emotionality that can no longer be controlled by the person or the company. The explanations are deliberately calculated to deceive, yet there is also a desperate attempt to give credibility and definitive form to a chaotic situation: to let words be the means of renewing contact with society.

But the social role built up by one character for himself is continually destroyed by another, devaluated into a sick sham existence that outsiders accept as real only out of pity. The image of an integral family, in which each member has his definite, unchallenged place, cannot be restored. There remains only a faulty, endlessly self-corrective outline of a life together that is constantly being threatened from within.

The problem of Ciampa from *Cap and Bells* is here repeated in a group of persons. The Frola-Ponza family is shown to be only an idiosyncratic construction, a substitute reality that drives underground a situation of potential danger to society.

But in this play the suppression is still more total, the situation still more unreal, because of duplication of the illusion. The playing becomes more and more stylized. With deliberate derision it displays its cheap and played-out methods. The meeting in the second act of the two crazy persons, which those present have arranged in order to find out "what is true and what is illusion," culminates in an eccentric display in which the overexcited wordless inner drama changes into comic parody. The action, "fast, anxious, tense with excitement," is an ironical combination of tragedy descending into melodrama. It reduces the play to its dramatic substratum—the explosive effect of fear and compassion.

Signora Frola acts the part of a deeply moved woman, playing on the drawing-room piano "an old melody, one of sweet melancholy and gracefulness," her daughter's favorite tune. ("But, as you know, since then, she cannot play any more. This is perhaps her worst grief. Poor child.") Ponza plays the part of a furiously angry man. In a state of almost animallike excitement, which almost paralyzes the overwhelmed Signora Frola, he listens as she acts out her madness for him. Then, ranting furiously, he insists on his own

madness: "Just as if she isn't dead." With infinite kind-
ness and sympathy she calms him, also moved to tears,
till he advances upon her threateningly: "Get out of
here. Go home. Go home!" Thereupon looking be-
seechingly at the company and sobbing, she leaves the
room. The group stands there looking at Ponza with
pity and terror.

But the real punchline comes at the end. Suddenly
Ponza removes his mask and explains quietly and
simply: "I had to do that. This is the only means by
which I can preserve her illusion. I have to shout the
truth to her face as if this were my mania." With this
kind of extreme illusion-making and breaking, Pirandello achieves what he wants to achieve in the theater
—the unexpected.

After Ponza's explanation they all stand spellbound
and silent, looking at each other. By creating this confusion in the people on the stage, Pirandello turns
them into a prototype of the people in the auditorium.
They can no longer assimilate the drama that is being
performed before their eyes as the drama of their own
crisis. It escapes them. They are only aware of its
external effects—a spectacular world of illusion, and
it shows that it is not the truth.

Pirandello continues playing out this dilemma till
all that remains is empty contradiction. He lets all
attempts to cast light on the matter by facts or docu-
ments shatter. (All evidence is said to have been lost
in the earthquake.) Finally he allows Signora Ponza,
the mysterious unknown of the play, to appear on the
stage.

It is no accident that of all persons it is Laudisi
who has the idea of getting Signora Ponza to make a

statement to the prefect. He belongs to both groups. On the one hand he is a member of the society he criticizes; but on the other he understands the behavior of the Frola-Ponza family, whose possession of a secret he defends because he ultimately doubts that it can be found out. "What, after all, can we really know about people? Who they are? What kind of people they are? What they do? Why they do it?"

Signora Ponza's appearance is proof of his skepticism. Her entrance like a dea ex machina is a spectacular piece of theater that brings the play to an abrupt end. Signora Ponza is the picture of a tragic heroine. Wearing deep mourning, she conceals her face by a thick, black, impenetrable veil. People make way for her. She walks rigidly forward. With a certain "somber pathos" she sends Signora Frola and Signor Ponza, who are hysterical with excitement, away. "Don't be afraid," she says to her husband. "Just go!" And the two of them go out weeping, whispering to each other in affectionate harmony.

Then, without lifting her veil, she tells the assembled company the truth: "I am the daughter of Signora Frola . . . and the second wife of Signor Ponza . . . and, as for me, I'm nobody!" But the prefect is perplexed: "But, signora, you can be but only one of the two."

To this her sibyl-like reply is: "No! I am the one for which you take me." And after looking at them through her veil for a moment, she leaves. This time, too, Laudisi has the last word: "And this, my friends, is the truth!" (With a look of derisive defiance at them all.) "Are you satisfied?" (He bursts out laughing.)

The end is abrupt, like all typical Pirandellian endings. But the transition from the particular to the general, from psychology to symbol, is no longer successful here. In the process it becomes distorted and veers toward the grotesque. Signora Ponza remains a hybrid —in part a tragic figure of domestic drama, in part a pseudo-philosophical abstraction. She is proof of the thesis advanced in the title and defended with mock seriousness by its apologist, Laudisi. Her appearance drives the real dramatic protagonists (Signora Frola and Signor Ponza) permanently from the stage. But it does not explain their story. Nor does it put anything in its place. It only states the story's secret and the impossibility of anyone ever getting to understand it.

Thus the play runs aground. But why? Pirandello left this question unanswered. His conclusion not only suppressed the real drama but also—by contrast with *Six Characters in Search of an Author*—all discussion of it. Signora Ponza's final sentence—"No! I am the one for which you take me"—is merely an assertion, a capricious leap from out of an enclosed inner world into an arbitrary outer one. Ultimately it proves nothing save the unspoken thesis of the play—that theater, and society, and the human mind in general, are not capable of understanding truth. That this is so is not explained intelligibly but only postulated as a basic fact.

To achieve this, Pirandello has to make the story of the Frola-Ponza family obscure to the point of incomprehensibility. He gives us practically nothing of his characters' history, offering them as victims of a catastrophe that has destroyed every trace of their past. Only thus was he able to permit his characters to create a world of illusion behind which the characters entrench themselves in order to prevent the outside world from catching any glimpse of their private lives. The analytical method used here, which Pirandello took from Ibsen, is destined to founder when applied to characters who insist on retaining their illusions. Pirandello employed it only to carry it ad absurdum, as a means of demonstrating the thesis that all explanations are useless. The process that is intended to uncover the hidden past only serves, by a strange irony, to make it all the more obscure.

But this is at the same time the beginning of a growing externalization. In refusing to allow anything on the stage to make sense, Pirandello emptied the story of meaning and reduced it to crude theatricality. Gesture, mimicry, dialogue, casting, and dramatic stereotypes all begin to take on an isolated and independent life of their own. It is this that makes the piece so playable, so fascinating. It can be acted with a total expressiveness that is partly psychological truth but partly sheer stage effect. The character types are firmly fixed, but by this very fact, as in the commedia dell'arte, they are made more flexible and open to spontaneous comedy.

In 1959 Claus Leininger put on in the theater at Göttingen a "production convincingly oscillating between the comic and the tragic, between caricature and pure humanity" (Claus-Henning Bachmann).

> The production gave fully exact and at the same time tense expression to all the nuances from pure situation comedy to almost tragic outbursts,

and released a precise and stormy fire of dialogue, which tore across the stage at an almost bewildering speed, with a superb vitality, perhaps a little too burlesque in detail and a little too crude in its contrasts, but rich in tension and impressively compact despite all nuances. [*Göttinger Presse*]

This is really the basic intention of the play. The obsessive delusions of the characters, which should jump out as the result of the constant breaking of the illusion, did not come through. The principal characters remained real and comprehensible in a grief that made them more humane and did not confine them to the eccentric ceremonial of their distorted, puppet-like existence. Margarete Andersen played Signora Frola, as a "half mysteriously ethereal, half despairingly tormented old woman." Signor Ponza (Klaus Behrendt) was "realistically inflammable" and hot-tempered. The rest of the company was also true to life. They displayed a "variegated collection of prudishly masked small-town weaknesses," humorously effective now and then, but lacking satirical sharpness.

It was in this play above all that Pirandello himself had stressed the absurd and grotesque. After his company performed this play at Frankfurt on 16 October 1925, Bernhard Diebold wrote: "In the course of this terrifying play we became convinced that both sides were equally crazy—and that all the other characters held their own in a quiet craziness of their own."

The performance was provocative in its complete unconcern, an unconcern that was carried to extremes. "It is bluff," cried one of the critics, furiously, "clever bluff at times—but bluff all the same. That's all it is, and nothing else!" Another regretted the "overvaluing of a playwright who could produce clever sketches." "What significance is there in our homage to a Hofmannsthal, a George, or a Thomas Mann," he asked reproachfully, "if we pay similar homage to Pirandello? In recognizing the inferior, we fail to honor the superior."

The critics did not understand that what was being performed was a bizarre tragic-comic puppet play with human actors: that material stuffed with profound psychological and philosophical meaning was being transformed into a joke that nevertheless maintained its claim to be considerably more than bluff. They did not understand why the small parts were "tastelessly exaggerated," why a man played an "elderly lady in the mask of Charley's Aunt," why a councilor was dressed "like a clerk on a very low wage."

But these were the farcical details that Pirandello thought important. They were meant to attract notice, meant to be ill-fitting or exaggerated, in order to pinpoint the mask. In this way the whole play veered toward the disordered and burlesque. Even the German critics were unable to deny that this shameless comedy playing was refreshing. It "sparkled," they found, "with animal life through the expressive strength of their active hands, arms, legs, and tongues."

The first American production of this play, under the title *Right You Are If You Think You Are*, was offered by the Theater Guild in February 1927. Directed by Philip Moeller, it cast Reginald Mason as

Lamberto Laudisi, Beryl Mercer as Signora Frola, Edward G. Robinson as Ponza, and Armina Marshall as Signora Ponza. Both the production and the drama won praise from Brooks Atkinson (*New York Times*, 24 February 1927), who wrote that the Guild had "mounted it with superb skill" and that it was a "production to be applauded."

About the play Mr. Atkinson wrote:

> Earnest playgoers, taxed beyond all bearing with the twisting of nice points, will complain that "Right You Are" is "a lot about nothing." And, of course, as Pirandello would consent, they are all right—so long as they think they are. But with no more substance than this fable to go upon, Pirandello manages to work up a passionate, comical rigmarole with a thousand penetrating intimations. To see the gossips gather, fight over the points, shift their loyalties from one person to the other, and to hear the placid comments of Pirandello's mouthpiece, Lamberto Laudisi, is to spend a pleasantly mad afternoon in the theater with no further reward. . . . With such stupid puppets to dangle on the threads of his drama, Pirandello runs from satire to metaphysics and on to melodrama, with no faltering steps. "Right You Are" is ingeniously exciting and amusing by turns.

Of this production, Gilbert W. Gabriel of the *Sun* assured theatergoers that this play was "primarily all of a brilliantly amusing comedy, a mesh of sly, sardonic mysteries which pull you in and keep you guessing fiercely to the end. . . . Certainly, of all his works which have been transported to New York none has been so beautifully and serenely skeptical as this, none has left the riddle of reality so satisfactorily unanswered."

Eric Bentley, in his notes to his own production of the play, also started out with this mixture of tragic hysteria and overheated comedy. The peculiarity of *Right You Are If You Think You Are* lies, in his eyes, precisely in the fact that in this play the sad and gloomy features that are clearly apparent in the Frola-Ponza story are also lurking, concealed, in the farcical aspects that make up the framework. Hysteria and madness are not too far below the surface.

Bentley saw farce above all in the peripheral parts played by the company, whereas in his view the appearances of the Frola-Ponza family come closer to tragedy. But decisive to both parts of the story is the rapid speed of the farce that grows out of the progressive repetition as a kind of mechanism similar to the uncannily rotating vehicles of an amusement ground. Thus he increases the play's pace and volume of sound in every act.

The playing of the two groups (the Frola-Ponza family and society) has to be different. One group has to play tragedy, with an impetuosity that has been long absent from the Anglo-American stage. The performance must not be based on psychological motivation. Ponza has to play violent emotion as such. From the assembled company Bentley required a comedy style that resembles vaudeville. Here too individual psychology must be eschewed, and attention directed to the ensemble playing. It was important to form "comic pairs" that can be variously interpreted by the performers.

The central comic figure was, in Bentley's view, Laudisi, who is a harlequin in modern dress. All his scenes are jokes. He is what the Italian stage calls a "diamond," and he is required to sparkle and glitter. He needs the fiery energy, the diabolic rhythm, that one thinks of in connection with the commedia dell'arte. In Bentley's production Laudisi has primarily a technical function. As connecting link between the comic chorus and the tragic trio, and also between the action on the stage and in the auditorium, he must be versed in all levels of acting, and must be able with flashing quickness to effect the transformation from the trivial to the serious, from tears to laughter.

But Bentley hinted that the play could also be interpreted in many other ways. He wrote that he would like to attempt a more naturalistic treatment one day. If he had at his disposal an ensemble of highly trained clowns, then he would also like to try a less naturalistic treatment. Here he envisaged a chorus of comic players, who leap up and sit down like jacks-in-the-box.

Eric Bentley's translation was used by the APA Repertory Company when they produced this play in November 1966 at the Lyceum Theater in New York City. One of the great actresses of our time, Helen Hayes, portrayed Signora Frola. Alternating with her in this role was Betty Miller. Stephen Porter directed.

In October 1972 the Roundabout Theater in New York City, a tiny, small-budget company, turned its hand to *Right You Are If You Think You Are*, using Eric Bentley's translation. The play and the production won high praise from Jerry Tallmer, drama critic on the *New York Post*. Calling the stage design of Holmes Easley—a wall of mirrors—a "perfect device,"

Stating his thesis clearly in the title, *Thus It Is (If It Seems So to You)*, Pirandello used the mode of drawing-room comedy to write a play that has been labeled, among other things, a social satire, an intellectual concept about the validity of illusions, a thoroughly delightful metaphysical melodrama. The American premiere, by the Theater Guild in New York City in 1927, under the title *Right You Are If You Think You Are*, directed by Philip Moeller, featured Edward G. Robinson (as Signor Ponza) and Beryl Mercer (as Signora Frola).

Through his very special insights into the nature of illusion and reality, Pirandello was able to portray madness so as to make it comprehensible. To escape from a reality of unhappiness and humiliation, Henry IV acts out the delusion of being a medieval German king for more than twenty years. Both these photographs illustrate his insistence that his servants enter into his private world. *Left*: Scene from the 1962 production offered at the Schauspielhaus in Bochum. Directed by Werner Düggelin, this production was a vehicle for the acting of Hurbert Suschka (as Henry IV, at left wearing mantle).

SCHAUSPIELHAUS, BOCHUM

Below: Scene from the version offered by the Piccolo Teatro of Milan in 1961, directed by Orazio Costa Giovangigli. The title role was played by Tino Carraro (in black robe, at left).

PICCOLO TEATRO, MILAN

A phantasmagoria, a medley of juggleries, a dream theater, *The Mountain Giants* expresses the plight of the modern world, a world in which fanaticism of all kinds has driven away the essentials by which men live.

Right: The unrivaled production of this play has been offered by Giorgio Strehler. Presenting the work as a magical, poetic dream play, a visionary spectacle, Strehler offered an interpretation only hinted at in the existing, incomplete text. In 1958 his unanimously well-received adaptation was performed at the Schauspielhaus in Düsseldorf. Ilse, the ill-fated countess, was played by Maria Wimmer; Cotrone, by Bernhard Minetti.

LISELOTTE STRELOW, BERLIN

Below: In 1966 Strehler offered it again at the Piccolo Teatro in Milan, with Valentina Cortese as Ilse (foreground, far right).

LUIGI CIMINAGHI, PICCOLO TEATRO, MILAN

Socha Pernon Inhau anew dator

One of the best-known, most influential plays in twentieth-century theater, *Six Characters in Search of an Author* is an innovative dramatization of the meaninglessness of private experience. In 1953 the play was produced by Oscar Fritz Schuh at the Kurfürstendamm Theater, Berlin. Here are the sketches for the stage setting and the costume design prepared by Caspar Neher, set and costume designer for many of the Brecht plays performed in the 1930s.

ROSEMARIE CLAUSEN, HAMBURG

In *Six Characters in Search of an Author*, Pirandello offered a family tragedy in which each of the four adults is obsessed with his own pain. This results in the death of the two children: the little girl, by drowning; the little boy, by suicide. In 1931 this play was premiered in America by the Bijou Theater in New York City. The scene above shows the Mother (as played by Doris Rankin), the Little Boy holding a gun (as played by Buddy Proctor), the Little Girl (as played by Bebe Gelhart).

he wrote that "this gave the show, from time to time, exactly the left-right reversal that 'Right You Are' and Pirandello are . . . all about." He gave high praise to the acting and wrote that in this production "director Gene Feist and his actors have hit almost exactly the right tone, bite, control."

The *New York Times* drama critic, Clive Barnes, wrote that he could "guardedly welcome" this production though his reservations about staging, direction, and acting were "mildly considerable." As to Pirandello's work, he wrote: "I find I approach his plays with a certain foreboding. They are clever but chilly, they so often heat the mind while leaving the heart unwarmed." In general he described it as "a play very well worth doing, and at the production's level worth seeing." He credited the company for using Eric Bentley's translation, which, he said, "has just the right primped and provincial seediness to it."

Douglas Watt voiced dislike for the entire venture. Though recognizing the performances of Dorothy Sands (as Signora Frola) and John LaGioia (as Signor Ponza) as effective, he described the disengagement of the audience as a result of "Gene Feist's fussy and stiff direction [which] makes lifeless caricatures" of the other roles.

The Pleasure of Honesty

CONTENTS: Angelo Baldovino, an eccentric nobleman who has come down in the world and has neither money nor credit, decides to marry a pregnant girl of good family, Agata Renni. By so doing he will get rid of his debts but also revenge himself on society. Immediately after the wedding, he demonstrates the kind of revenge he has in mind. He becomes a domestic tyrant, who plays the role of respectable husband and father to show up the weaknesses of others. He fulfills the demands of respectability to an exaggerated degree, and requires the same behavior from his wife, his mother-in-law, and the married lover of his wife. The tyranny of respectability soon becomes unbearable, and Fabio, his rival, decides to get rid of Baldovino by framing him for theft.

But Baldovino sees through the strategem and turns it against his enemy. He agrees to leave. But he insists that Fabio actually do the stealing, and only then shift the blame on him. This turns Fabio into the villain and Baldovino into the innocent victim. His wife's love now turns to him, even as he himself takes the money from the till, in order to force Fabio, who still hesitates, to put an end to the dishonorable marriage situation. For in the meantime Baldovino has discovered that he has blood in his veins, and that it is time to save his own honor, at least in his own eyes. This turns him into a human being and wins him his wife, with whom he had previously only lived in a sham marriage. She is prepared to go with him and stay with him without considerations of honor.

When Pirandello toured Germany in the autumn of 1925 with the Teatro d'Arte, their repertory included *Six Characters in Search of an Author*, *Henry IV*, *Thus It Is*, and *The Pleasure of Honesty*. It was an indication of the importance Pirandello attached to *The Pleasure of Honesty*, for by that time he had already written thirty plays. The performance in Berlin's Staatstheater was disappointing. After an earlier successful staging at the Reinhardt Theater, people expected a glittering display of clowning, a comedy play. Instead they were given a presentation of verbal dialogue that was oversentimentalized and sluggish.

The story was lost under the words. Pirandello had not cut a word of the text that now hung heavily in the foreground, slowing up the play and shaping it into a tragedy rather than a comedy.

Yet there is hidden in this play a comedy, a drawing-room comedy, with a blissfully happy ending and a hero who only simulates wickedness but is repaid with good because he is himself good. Few of Piran-

dello's plays are so free of tragic contradictions, so
much a play of utopian wish fulfillment. All is bliss:
love triumphs over reason, life over form, the individual over society.

Behind the grotesque mask that Baldovino wears,
there is no other. Here a heart is beating, and Agata,
his wife, sets it free. Truth is suddenly revealed as a
simple fact of love and happiness. And even the small
absurd flourish with which Pirandello usually disfigures
his dreams turns into an embellishment for once. The
gesture at the end with which Agata hands the handkerchief to Baldovino, who is overcome with emotion,
only calls for sympathy; it is humanly beautiful—a
sign of a reconciled, a better world.

It was this quality that probably led Pirandello to
alter the mood of the play, to lade it with a heavily
thoughtful, melancholy gravity, for its performance.
The achievement of a universal harmony must have
seemed highly suspect to him. It precisely presented
the "idealistic simplification and harmonious logic of
facts and characters" that he despised in the "average
writer."

But in its dialogue the play reveals a superstructure
in which the real Pirandellian theme comes fully to
expression. Baldovino is the typical Pirandellian hero,
whose drama is primarily one of words. Fabio himself
admits that Baldovino's gift of words is fascinating.
Like the others, he is scarcely able to follow Baldovino's head-whirling arguments.

The moment Baldovino appears in the first act, and
confronts Fabio, he begins to construct his own and
his opponent's masks. He tells Fabio that this is una-
voidable. He puts on his eyeglasses, behind which, as

with Ciampa, there lies concealed a piercing eye. And he develops, point by point, the part each will have to play.

> "What do I have to do? Nothing. I only represent. The deed—no very beautiful one—is done by you. You have already done it. And I have to put it right again. You will repeat it, and once more I shall hush it. But in order to be able to do this, I must ask for your respect—in your own interest and above all in the signora's interest. To give it to me in the position you now find yourself in will not be easy for you. But I ask it, not for myself personally but for what I embody— the highly regarded husband of a society lady."

The suggestion seems harmless enough. But Baldovino makes quite clear what he means by it—the destruction of identity. Not only his own but that of his rival. He makes himself into a formula of abstract and absolute respectability, and turns Fabio, whose social function he himself exercises, into an instinct-bound animal. This gives him power, the power of a social prejudice that he exploits and assaults until it shows itself for what it is—a construction hostile to life.

Baldovino isolates the principle of honor and metamorphoses it into a weapon against those who demand it from him. He turns into a tyrant who expects very heavy sacrifices from others: he stands for an oppressive reduction of freedom and requires the observance of all abstract forms of social life. This total identification with morality is for Pirandello the most radical expression of antisocial protest.

"You cannot imagine," Baldovino insists, "with what pleasure I revenge myself on a society that refuses to honor my signature on anything." The credit, the liberty, that society refuses him he takes for himself by fulfilling the demands made by society to the point at which they become meaningless, thus destroying them. This is his revenge. But it turns him into a slave of his ideas. "I live most pleasurably in the absolute of an abstract formula," he says in the second act, in justification of his luxurious life. But only his body appears to be there; he himself is perishing in nothing but calculations and speculations, all for the benefit of others. Nothing belongs to him. The formula sets him free, but the price is his life.

This "freedom" that Baldovino evolves with revengeful spirit is projected by a long and ponderous exposition the purpose of which is more to support Pirandello's ideas than to get the story moving. Nevertheless, this is where the play's dramatic impulse lies, its point of attack.

The second act deals with the problem of ironic adaptation, but its dramatic strength lies only in words. We are told that Baldovino's pedantic correctness irritates those close to him, that he is hated and intrigued against. Fabio and the members of the board of directors, whose chairman he has become with Fabio's help, want to unseat him. He knows this and evolves further evil plans. If he is put out on the street he intends to take with him the son who is his in the eyes of the law and to pull this son with him into the abyss.

"You know," he says to Maurizio, "how malicious I can be. There is a beast lowering inside me. I wanted to free myself of it and chain it up. That is why I entered into the agreement they offered me here. You must respect it exactly as I wanted it. For who knows what I am capable of if a time should come when I am no longer bound by it."

One anticipates the worst. But the threat remains an idle one. The drama takes place only in the mind. The result is comedy that points up the smallest, most trifling details of the conflict so exhaustively talked through. Baldovino insists, against the will of the rest of the family, in giving the son the bombastic name Sigismondo. "A ponderous, ugly name" it is, as he himself agrees, but the name is traditional in his family. And since he must give the child a name, it can be only this name, so that outward forms are preserved.

This is a harmless joke, an act of revenge purely comic in effect. The indignant family is speechless and caricatures the scene in dumb show. The mother-in-law falls motionless into a chair. Fabio sits down as well and puts his clenched fists on his knees. Maurizio also seats himself, shaking his head and sighing audibly. There is a long silence, Pirandello notes, that the actors can precipitate into the grotesque.

Pirandello, it goes without saying, wants more here, too, than merely jesting and laughing. Behind the absurdities of his humor there must, he insisted, appear something serious and painful. But this play lacks that dark, all-pervading emotion that usually overstates or paralyzes the action, thereby indicating that what is taking place on stage is not simply comic but grotesque and double-edged as well. The joke, it is true, has a serious and even, in intention, a tragic theme. But as it is carried out it remains banal. It is nothing more than the revenge of an outsider who angers the establishment, which a blunder has put at his mercy.

The Austrian critic Alfred Polgar was right when he wrote that Baldovino, that epitome of respectability, is a born comical figure of fun who can transcend himself in thought but not in act. His drama remains nonexistent, because Pirandello does not permit it to happen. "Pirandello's fire continues to lack dramatic force," Polgar said. But it is not "fire" that is lacking. It is intention. Giving his plays dramatic edge was not beyond Pirandello's power, as he showed in other plays. But this time he eschewed it. He pulled Agata over to Baldovino's side. When Baldovino, with "reverence and a feeling for propriety," as the priest described it, wants the child's baptism to take place in the church instead of the house, she agrees with him.

"You have agreed with him from the very first day he was brought into this house," Fabio accuses her. Fabio has been refused his lover's rights from that day on. "You are on his side," he complains. To which she replies, "I am my own woman." It comes to the same thing. Baldovino gives back to Agata her sense of direction, her respect for him and for herself. The world regains its proper balance. Through Baldovino, Agata discovers a new way of life. Through her, he discovers life itself.

The totally contradictory elements usually found in Pirandello's work are here reconciled. Even Fabio, who throws money, for which no accounting has to be done, into Baldovino's way, in order to tempt him to embezzlement, can achieve nothing with his intrigue. The result is predetermined. Baldovino is the victor. Evil leaves him untouched. He wins the test and thereby earns, as in a fairy story, the hand of the wife whom he loves.

Why Pirandello let himself so unreservedly indulge in high hopes in this play is not clear. But it surely indicates something. It reveals to us his most intimate expectations, those on which he was usually silent because his conscious mind would not let him recognize that he believed in them. His experience belied such optimistic expectations. He learned that between men there could be only fear, conflict, and at most pity—but never trust. All the more passionately did he seek for the opposite, which he knew to be impossible, and which he therefore suppressed.

To bring this marvel undiluted onto the stage is an illogicality that transcends every rule of Pirandellian theater. Or so it seems. But perhaps it is also the other way round. It may be that just a utopia is the true motivation for a dramatist who so unambiguously rejects all hope.

*Six Characters
in Search of an Author*

CONTENTS: In the stage directions Pirandello wrote that this play had no acts or scenes. Nor does it have a plot in the ordinary sense of the word. It is a play that has to be constructed by the players. Six stage characters—Father, Mother, Son, Stepdaughter, Little Boy, Little Girl—appear before the director, who is on the point of rehearsing a Pirandello play, and beg him to let them perform their own tragedy. Their drama is on two levels: the melodramatic family story, which they act out in their roles, and the tortured awareness that their story is incomplete.

They are passionately anxious to complete the play that their author planned out but then discarded, in order to free themselves from it. Slowly, in close discussion with the director, with the actors, and among themselves, they develop their play. We learn the story, piece by piece.

Years ago the father had forced the mother to live with another man. He claims that he did this out of

76

pity because he believed they were better suited to each other than he and his wife were. He had arranged, however, for his son to grow up healthily in the country. After the second man's death the impoverished mother returned from abroad with three illegitimate children. At this point the drama begins. The father, who knows nothing of their return, meets his stepdaughter, in the shop of Madame Pace, a procuress, whose atelier is a front for a brothel. He begins to proposition her, but suddenly recognizes her. At this point the mother comes in and finds the two of them.

In the confusion that follows, the family, which has returned to live with the father, falls totally apart. Each of them is only concerned with himself and his own problems—the father with his guilt; the stepdaughter with her hatred; the mother with her horror, consumed with her longing for the son of her first marriage; the son, who withdraws from them all, full of contempt and indifference. For the two children this general confusion turns out to be fatal—the little girl drowns, the little boy shoots himself. The two dramatic moments—the seduction scene at Madame Pace's and the death of the two children—are the focal points of the tragedy that is to be enacted.

But the play is a failure. The six characters cannot perform together because they are unable to distance themselves from the events; and the actors who are meant to act the scenes after them do not succeed because they lack the immediacy of the emotional experience. The performance does not achieve the required balance of mounting fear. It ends with the suicide of the boy. This is something that cannot be improvised. It appears once again as a terrible fact. The actors thereupon disappear from the stage. Only the six characters move once more like shadows along a screen faintly illuminated by a green light.

The first performance of *Six Characters in Search of an Author* was one of the greatest theatrical sensations of the century. It took place in Rome on 10 May 1921, and became a cause célèbre of the kind that would be practically unimaginable today. Audience, actors, and critics fought on the stage. The audience gathered together after the performance, threatened Pirandello, and continued discussing the play for hours on end in the public places of the city.

A few months later, when the play was put on in Milan, indignation was replaced by enthusiasm. And through the next three years the play was successful on stages in every country of the world. In 1922 it was put on in London and New York; in 1923 Georges Pitoëff mounted his famous production in Paris; and in 1924 Max Reinhardt staged the play in Berlin.

The influence of this play is still unequaled. It not only impressed fellow dramatists like G. B. Shaw and Antonin Artaud but also impelled a practical man such as John Ford to finance an American tour for Pirandello, because he thought that a tour by Pirandello, a "man of the people," would be a commercial success. This drama, that shows most clearly its own impossibility, is not only the most dramatic of Pirandello's plays but one of the most dramatic plays of all time. The reason is its immediacy, which Pirandello does not for once exhaust or reason away, but to which he returns again through the detour of a double fiction.

In admitting from the start that his characters are character parts, incomplete creatures of a dramatic moment, he restores to them the entire burden of experience, to which they remain tied and which therefore they are not able to exhaust. They speak and act under the compulsion of awareness of their roles—an awareness that knows nothing except the trauma of its emotion. Every word, every movement, every action, thus necessarily is a fragment of compelling direct drama.

There has been much speculation about the origin of *Six Characters*, not least by Pirandello himself. Nine years after the play was first put on, he tried to explain its meaning in an extended foreword. But the result, influenced by the views of the critics, betrays more about the discoveries he himself was able to make later when he thought about the play quietly than about the original motivation for its creation.

The story appears to have come to Pirandello from out of a mystical darkness, like a miracle, a spontaneous illumination of the imagination. He did not discuss his curious obsession with this dramatic material in which he himself could find no meaning but which he could not drive out of his mind. It is quite clear that he did not manage to discover a meaning in *Six Characters*. It is not so obvious why he was so fascinated by this material.

What was he to do with the story of a family disaster that, looked on objectively, was both private and contrived? Nevertheless, from the moment the characters appear on the stage, there can be no doubt that they have a real story to tell. Their emotion seems genuine, and this is only possible because Pirandello himself identifies with them and takes their feelings seriously, even such feelings as he rejects. Through all the distortions and ironic fragmentations of the play, one recognizes that its basis lies in a personal experience, which Pirandello tried vainly to objectify. The foreword has something to say about this:

> Without wanting to, without knowing it, in the strife of their bedeviled souls, each of them [the characters], defending himself against the accusations of the others, expresses as his own living passion and torment the passion and torment that for so many years have been the pangs of my spirit: the impossibility of mutual understanding that is irrevocably based on the empty definition of words; the multiple personality that each of us has corresponding to the possibilities of being to be found in each of us; and finally the inherent tragic conflict between life (which is always moving and changing) and form (which holds it immutable).

The impossibility of understanding himself was only one cause of the pangs of spirit assailing Pirandello; the realities of his daily life made no small contribution to his pain. The efforts made for decades to come to some kind of understanding with his sick wife, whether through logical arguments or through pity, ended in failure in the same year, 1917, in which he first planned his *Six Characters*. (Initially it was conceived of as a novel.)

In an attack of fury his wife accused him of incest with his own daughter. At this the daughter fled the house, refusing to return. The family life, held together so long and with such efforts, finally collapsed. Pirandello's wife had to be taken to a sanatarium, from which she was never released. To understand the underlying tale, which Pirandello then deliberately distorted, these events should be related directly to the play.

The unhappiness in his own home oppressed him and filled him with the compulsion to objectify it in a story that embodied the meaninglessness of his private experience. Here was drama. He himself had experienced it—the hysterical excesses, the horror of the breakup of a personality. Here is the estrangement between people who think they know each other and suddenly find themselves enemies, see themselves making incredible accusations and vainly trying to justify themselves.

Pirandello must have clearly seen the dramatic effectiveness of such a situation. He observed it, and it worked in him, but he could find no way of portraying it. The subject was weighed down by a taboo. He felt prohibited from revealing the sufferings of himself and his family, his own sad family story. He also doubted whether such intimate emotions could be transferred to the realm of general validity.

As a "philosophical writer," it was never enough for Pirandello, as he wrote in the foreword to this play, "to present a man or a woman and what is special and characteristic about them simply for the pleasure of portraying them; to narrate a particular affair, lively or sad, simply for the pleasure of narrating it." He was a writer who used only characters and events "that have been soaked, so to speak, in a particular sense of life and acquire from it a universal value."

His own experience did not yield this sense of life. He kept on rearranging his material until it seemed to yield a general problem. In the tragedy of the six characters, the family disturbance is not the result of an illness, but the consequence of a fragmented, no longer restrained consciousness. It is the father who artificially breaks up the family, obsessed by the demon of experiment. He takes the son away from his mother and gives him to a peasant woman in the country, so that he will grow up healthy and strong in natural surroundings. For the same reason, he explains, he had married the mother because she was a poor and humble woman.

Pirandello considered it madness to construct a life in which basic relationships are altered according to a presumably more rational, more moral scheme. Perhaps, says the father, it's crazy, but what can one do? "All my life I have had these wretched longings for a certain moral hygiene." These aspirations gave him the idea to mate his own wife with his secretary because they understood each other so well. And only by means of this detour does the father succeed in reestablishing contact with life.

"I watched with the most tender care the new family that grew up around her," he tells us. "The thought of them began gradually to fill up the emptiness I felt all around me. I wanted to know that they were living a peaceful life concerned with only the simplest things of existence. That they were happy because they were not affected by the complicated thoughts that tormented me."

But this exaggerated sentimental interest in the simple life only drives them further apart. It scares away the secretary, who takes the family abroad. The mother and children return, unknown to anyone, only after his death. The father, driven by long years of loneliness to the brothel, and the stepdaughter, whose fatherless situation led her to become a prostitute, meet at the house of a procuress and recognize each other in their distorted, antisocial roles. This results in feelings of hatred and guilt and a permanent crisis of trust. A new existence together becomes impossible. The whole meaning of family life is perverted. The family now no longer protects life but destroys it. The two children of the family, left to themselves in the general confusion, die.

The story is clear and logical in intention. Pirandello wants an accounting with himself, the accounting with a consciousness that flees from the old norms, yet remains tied to them, thus encouraging a life-threatening anarchy. But this is not the stuff of drama. The story is an epic one, generated by an unusual psyche.

The approach to the climax is slow and ponderous. It is constructed out of a number of differentiated modes of behavior that bring about the catastrophe—although without dramatic inevitability. The meeting of the father and stepdaughter, the death of the children, are artificially contrived and do not provide a satisfactory method for projecting a personal experience that cannot, despite all efforts, express itself dramatically.

In its fatal mixture of unsubtle outer effects and difficult inner events, it is a monstrous theatrical conception. The characters pursued Pirandello, without, however, having the backing of any kind of story.

They chose certain moments of the day, he wrote in his foreword, to tempt him by suggesting this or that scene and indicating the effects that could be achieved by them, the fresh interest an unusual situation might arouse, and so on.

We have to take all this literally. In effect, the story kept on coming back to Pirandello because he could not dispel it from his mind. It stayed, asserting itself obstinately, without form or cohesion, a dramatic impulse with its own inner justification. Thus it became a new theatrical experience for Pirandello. The original unwanted idea repeated itself on a higher plane where it was taken up in a double sense—discarded and thereby revalidated in its struggles with the demands made by the theater.

What Pirandello was now concerned with was no longer his personal conflict only but the conflict of the theater itself. A second theme superimposed itself on the first. The broken relationships between the characters returned, more radical and more basic, in the disturbed mediation of the play. Form and matter were no longer identical. Individual experience and the mechanics of the stage confronted each other as contradiction and resulted in a new drama.

What was previously impossible in this play now becomes possible. The epic exposition acquires a dramatic function because the action is laid on an earlier date. We see it in the making and hear it discussed. What the six characters bring onto the stage is no longer a closed story but a discarded play—a drama only hinted at, lacking all shape and form, violently foreshortened, chaotic, constantly interrupted, full of digressions and contradictions. And what confronts them is the untidy, worn-out apparatus of the theater, with its mechanisms, tricks, and routines, and its members—the actors and the director.

Both sides try to "make" the play. The characters try to present their unfinished story, and the actors to transform it into a finished performance by reenacting the scenes.

Thus the play becomes more and more diffuse. Epic material enters into the story, as narration, reflection, and commentary. The characters constantly explain themselves, defend themselves, accuse one another. They discuss their early history in detail, their motives and feelings, until the director interrupts to remind them that the whole thing is, after all, only narration.

The play they are to perform shrinks to small, fragmentary episodes. They rehearse two scenes—the scene at Madame Pace's establishment and the scene in the garden culminating in the death of the two children. But of the first scene there remain only the flowery phrases and gestures of greeting between father and stepdaughter. And in the second scene the entire action turns into a passionate self-justification by the characters. Self-awareness and emotion thrust their way in everywhere, dramatize the drama yet again, and break it up into small episodes. Emotional outbursts and theoretical discussions, stage directions and disputes, stage effects and actors' talk, all intermingle, changing into new and independent elements that combine to make the play into a curious kind of collage.

In place of a single entity the play dissolves in fragments that break up the main action into a constantly changing succession of ever newer, smaller episodes. Their effectiveness lies in those areas where dramatic techniques collide with the drama of the characters. This results in short circuiting, in a rapid transition from the comic to the tragic, from the naturalistic to the grotesque, from the overstylized to the coarsely spontaneous. Dramatic effects and techniques are heaped on one another, vie with one another, and finally destroy one another.

In order to achieve an utter climax, Pirandello constructed the play entirely out of the trivialities of stage preparations. "When the audience enters the theater, the curtain is raised and the stage is almost dark and empty, so that from the very beginning one gets the impression of a performance not quite ready."

As soon as the auditorium is dark, the property man appears in working clothes, fetches some boards, and begins to nail them up. The play starts at this, the most banal, most illusionless moment on any stage, and continues in a series of leaps to keep pace with, and overtake, the constant change in the level of reality. The property man makes way for the stage manager, who wants to set up the scene for the rehearsal of Pirandello's play, *Role Playing*. The actors enter, talk to each other, smoke, dance. The director follows, and they discuss the rehearsal. But before it begins, the doorkeeper brings in the six characters. With their appearance, naturalism turns into illusion.

The six characters—unlike the actors—leave us in no doubt about their artificiality. Their appearance is stylized. They wear stiffly draped costumes, making them look almost statuelike, and masks. They bring with them a sense of magic. When the stage manager, at the request of the director, wants to get them off the stage, he is inhibited by a curious fear. The step-daughter sings a coquettish song, and the actors, as though drawn by a strange magic, move toward her, putting forth their hands slightly to seize hold of her.

It is only this magic that makes the play possible. But at the same time it paralyzes the actors because it evokes in them the desire to possess the same magic.

Step by step the six characters force their way onto the stage. They tell their story, act it out, analyze it, and are repeatedly forced to a stop by a powerful excitement whose real reason remains unknown. But it is the cause of their magic; it moves the play forward and finally also leads to its failure. For the magic that surrounds them is only the aura of the experiences they have not been able to overcome, and over which the stage has no power.

That is why the play turns into a lifeless imitation when it is played by actors who want to fashion the stuff of life into material for the stage. The characters' attempt, on the other hand, to tell the whole truth about their tragedy culminates in sheer terror. The seduction scene improvised by the father and the step-daughter ends abruptly with the horrified cry of the mother, which makes the director shrink back as far as to the footlights. And the second scene ends with the revolver shot that not only performs again the death of the boy but makes it happen all over again. In the general confusion the actors are driven from the stage for good.

The entire drama of the six characters is contained in this unarticulated moment of shock. Their traumatic fate is to be chained to it and always to have to repeat it. They try all the more urgently to put it into words and so to free themselves from the unbearable tension of its emotional pressures. But the only result is a crude violence that flashes through the play like lightning and constantly forces it back to the point of its beginning—a hysterical, speechless confusion.

The six characters suffer, like the heroes of other Pirandello plays, from the extreme introverting and subjectivity of their story, which cannot be encompassed by any of the conventional theatrical modes. But in contrast to those other Pirandellian characters who express their conflict only in a pseudo fashion and by a seeming adaptation, the six characters are fighting for a radical liberation from their personal problems.

This turns them into declared critics of the theater. Externally, the usual constellation of a Pirandellian drama is repeated: people who have lost their social bearings and act out their conflict before a group of socially unblemished spectators (in this case the actors). But this time they insist on portraying the full extent of their personal drama in the face of every compulsion to adapt and stylize it. They insist on the uniqueness and noninterchangeableness of their personal destiny, on an individualization that transcends all the theater's powers to communicate it.

When the stepdaughter is about to perform the scene in Madame Pace's atelier, she wants to take off her clothes, for this is what really happened. The director's objection—one can't have this kind of thing on the stage ("Even truth has its limits")—fills her with indignation. "What you want to do is to piece together a little sentimental romantic scene made out of my repulsion, out of all the reasons, that make me what I have become—one reason more terrible and

vulgar than another—you want to make it into a sentimental piece of crap. But I want to act my tragedy,
my own tragedy."

Peter Szoudi has suggested, in his *Theory of the
Modern Drama*, that here, in the stepdaughter's protest, naturalism was attempting to break through. But
it is a different kind of naturalism from the photographic truth to life of the actors. The demand for
truth and reality, which the six characters make, is an
attack on the pose of a routinely externalized naturalism and sets against it a naturalism of inner truth, a
ruthless exposure of life stunted and oppressed by
taboos.

The six characters want "life" itself, total reality
that does not omit any detail however intimate. But
this leads to the same mechanistic performance on the
stage that is the object of their attack. In their radical-
ism they want to reenact only the raw material, the
unchanged emotional stuff of their drama. In the end
this leads only to a reification of the play. The six
characters demand an overexact reproduction of their
scenes from the actors; they insist on literal exactness
of dialogue, a photographic imitation of their gestures.
They find fault with the decor because the backcloth
is striped, not, as in reality, white. They criticize the
play in general because it is not life. And they try
desperately to perfect the imitation of external reality
to such an extent that life itself may spring out from
it.

Pirandello saw where this led. He forced this supra-
naturalness to the point where it ultimately changes
into its opposite, into a grotesque arbitrariness, in
which stage properties acquire their own independ-

ence and create a new and higher reality from out of themselves.

In the seduction scene the photographically repro-duced stage decor conjures up Madame Pace herself in the form of a stylized, puppetlike figure. The father fills the set with the hats and coats of her dressmaker's atelier and makes them seem so true to life that she herself appears as if called up by the ambience of her shop. "Perhaps," says the father, "if we arrange the stage here as precisely as possible, who knows, maybe Madame Pace will be attracted by the very appurte-nances and the ambience of her trade and will appear among us."

The father invites the actors to look toward the exit at the back of the stage. "There. Just look!" he shouts. The door at the back of the stage is thrown open, and Madame Pace takes a few steps forward. "She is a fat old creature with a monstrous reddish-blond wig, in which a flaming red rose is worn on one side in the Spanish fashion. Heavily made up, she is in full rig. She wears an elegant dress of red silk. In one hand she carries a fan of ostrich feathers; in the other hand, which is raised, she has a burning cigarette."

With the monstrously got up figure of Madame Pace appearing out of nowhere, the play moves for a moment into the realm of the absurd. Breaking loose from the tensions engendered by the constricting framework of the theater, it makes a powerful leap into the unfettered world of the imagination and achieves a sovereignty of its own, a flexibility as spon-taneous as that of imagination itself.

"When I had the thought of letting Madame Pace

come into existence on the stage," Pirandello justified himself in his foreword, "I felt that I was able to do it and I did it. . . . Because, contrary to the deceptive appearance, this fantastic birth is brought into a mysterious, organic, relationship to the entire play."

Ionesco was to argue with noticeable similarity thirty years later: "I for my part have made up my mind to adhere to no rules other than those of the powers of my imagination. . . . The true nature of things, truth itself, can only be revealed to us by the power of the imagination that is more real than any reality." Madame Pace, too, is more realistic than any reality, as the father points out to the protesting actors:

> "But excuse me, all of you! Why do you want, because of a trivial truth, to destroy this miracle of a higher reality, a miracle that became visible, conjured up by the ambience of the scene. It has a better right to live here than all of you, because it is much truer than you are. Which actress will be able to present Madame Pace like this? This, here, is Madame Pace."

Pirandello had clearly seen that the theater of the absurd might be able to gain a new mastery over the stage through the free play of the imagination. But he introduced this idea only to reject it. He held Madame Pace up to ridicule. The peculiar jargon, half Italian, half Spanish, spoken by this grotesque apparition, evokes loud laughter among the actors.

The mother's horrified indignation finally drives Madame Pace off the stage altogether. As she plays the procurer scene and suggests the father as a possible client for the stepdaughter, the mother rushes up to her with the cry "You witch, you witch! You murderer!" Then she tears off her wig.

In the confrontation of the two characters Pirandello calls his own play in question. The two of them can't be here together, says the father. Also Pirandello thinks this impossible. The grotesque and the tragic exclude each other. The humane aspect retains its dominance: it is stronger than the tricky filmlike abandonment of convention. Pirandello thereby suppresses as it were his own anarchic leanings.

Madame Pace is a procurer. In her dressmaker's atelier she serves the ladies of better society; in her back room she panders to rich men. She serves society, but surreptitiously she breaks it up. Pirandello recognized this same tendency in his own dramas. He too placed himself at the service of society, but at the same time pulled it into the abyss.

The freedom that has emancipated itself from all traditional bourgeois ties tempted him. But it also appalled him. Fear of sliding into an uncontrollable morass bound him to society and to the traditional forms of the bourgeois theater. But at the same time it drove him away from those forms. It is the horror of the ever-widening consciousness that renders all relations relative—a horror that can neither be dispelled nor calmed by any socially accepted form.

Pirandello cannot free himself from this tension. The play continues to move from trick to tragedy, and back again, but does not come down firmly on either side. Again and again, Pirandello tries in vain to gain mastery over the drama by means of contrivances and

devices, to destroy its magic by betraying the techniques of illusion.

Thus in the garden scene he explained the entire
hocus-pocus of theatrical effects. He lets the audience
watch how the magical scenery is erected on the stage
—a garden in the evening in bluish moonlight. And
so it loses its magic. It begins to look comic. The
cypresses float down from the rigging loft; a white
backcloth appears as sky; a blue spotlight creates the
moonlike atmosphere.

But these ironic stage effects do nothing to stop the
inexorable approach of terror. The two youngest children die in the garden. This too can be made to look
like a cheap effect. Nevertheless, something of the terrible reality comes through: something of the terror
Pirandello felt when facing his compulsive view of
a totally insecure world, one in which children become
victims of social derailment.

This shock brings the improvised play to a halt. The
story remains behind, incomplete as before. At the
end the outlines of the characters can be seen gliding
like searching, unredeemed shadows over a greenish-lit
backcloth. They appear once more on the night-blue
stage. The stepdaughter runs off and breaks out in
shrill laughter.

What is new in *Six Characters*, and unrepeatable
in this form, is the theater's own self-awareness carried
to the point of destruction. The play within the play
as a means of breaking through illusion, of a paradoxical and parodistic self-criticism, is a well-tried theatrical device. It can be found in the baroque theater as
well as the commedia dell'arte and the romantic theater.

Pirandello made this device his starting point. But in his play the real dramatic theme turns out to be the debate of the theater with itself. The play shows us, with increasing self-awareness, the progress of its own inner crisis. Thus it learns not only to recognize its limits but also to enlarge them. In trying to distance itself from the traditional theater of illusion, it becomes ever more theatrical. In a single developmental leap it discovers in essence all the possibilities of the modern theater. It tries out didactic theater, theater of the absurd, stylized theater, expressionistic drama. But only in order to reject them all immediately.

The entire performance is a single once-and-for-all sellout of all dramatic styles, which puts a stop to any further drama. Nevertheless, Pirandello continued to write, and the reason for this seeming inconsistency lies in the impossibility of the attempt. For it is only impossible because it cannot take the time to indulge in exhibitionism. That is why the play does not come to an end, even when the curtain falls. It is continued in Pirandello's subsequent plays, all of which, with an almost obsessive compulsion, attempt the same thing: to make their protest against form as form.

Pirandello knew this to be impossible. But what impelled him continually to try and fail again is the ambiguity of his original dramatic experience—the urge to dissolve all forms and the horror this brought with it. This is a mythical experience that seeks a dramatist—that is, a consciousness clarifying such experience.

Pirandello and the company of the Teatro d'Arte were billed at the Berlin Staatstheater from 12 to 14

October 1925. On the program were three plays—*Six Characters in Search of an Author*, *Henry IV*, and *The Pleasure of Honesty*. On 30 December 1924, Max Reinhardt had put on the *Six Characters*, with phenomenal success. The critics now came, on that first evening, to make comparisons. The audience was prejudiced. Berlin was rated as the theatrical capital of the world, Reinhardt as a brilliant and internationally famous theatrical innovator. The Italians, on the other hand, were thought of as naive, merry little theater people, who had no idea of the complexities of the art of staging and producing plays that had recently been developed and refined to the highest degree.

The verdict was as expected. Pirandello's production was found to be "primitive," the playing of the principal parts "scarcely better than a good average." Julius Meyer-Graefe, who pronounced the most destructive judgment, arrogantly ridiculed the sprightliness of the people from the Teatro d'Arte: "Be happy, laugh, dance, amuse yourselves, be as unstable as possible! When you have acquired our stability and are capable of putting on a play like this according to all the rules of theatrical art, then you will stop laughing."

The Germans were disturbed to find that the Italians did not treat the play as seriously as they did themselves. Reinhardt, they insisted, had brought out the "human and tragic" elements. Under his direction the play had "experienced an extraordinary deepening, revealing the secrets of the soul's complexities" (Franz Köppen). In Pirandello's production one missed the "special devices and nuances," the pauses, the psychology of the "movements, groupings, positionings." With him there was no dark background, the lighting effects confined themselves to the contrast between bright and dark, everything was overly clear in its outlines, more obvious in its effects, on a stage that was totally open and was joined to the auditorium by means of steps at the side. The "secrets of the stage" seemed with him to be secrets no longer.

It was acknowledged, however, that the terseness and openness of the play, with its "storm of gesticulations" and "whirlwind of talk" seemed both more concentrated and more "real" (Alfred Klaar). The critics also praised the disciplined, unified ensemble playing. In Pirandello's company there were no stars; each actor had to fit in with the total conception of the play. In spite of this, the performances of Marta Abba and Picasso stood out.

> The father, Lamberto Picasso, and the stepdaughter, Marta Abba . . . emerged more and more clearly from out of their shadowy existence into stormy, eccentric, passionate life. Whereas Picasso's first appearance reminded them [the Germans] of their own Gülstorff as he worked his way out of the darkness in embarrassment and shyness, as the action progresses his excitement grows ever wilder, and Marta Abba keeps pace with his unbridled emotions and the revelation of her deep-seated feelings. [Alfred Klaar]

The father and the stepdaughter were, in Pirandello's eyes, the central figures of the play. For this reason they were given from the beginning a quite different reality by Pirandello than by Reinhardt, who placed the director in the forefront and turned the six characters into a director's vision.

Pallenberg, who played the part of the director in Reinhardt's production, had his back turned to the audience during the entire play and thus forced the play into a new perspective. The six characters moved into an imaginary world, and the figure of the director also remained "surrounded with a shudder of unreality." Pallenberg, the critics asserted, had brought to the part "more heart than did the dramatist himself." He had enriched it with his sensibility, changed the performance from loudness to softness. Whereas at the beginning he had come across as fidgety and jumpy, his playing became increasingly inward, still and spellbinding, expressive of a secret horror, once he was confronted by the needs of the six characters.

For Pirandello, on the other hand, the director, played by Egisto Olivieri, remained of secondary importance. He was "all officiousness, adroit flexibility, professional zeal." He presented the image of what a director is assumed to be. The mother (Jone Frigerio) too took a less important place in Pirandello's production. She did not, in her timidity, as Alfred Klaar wrote, "reveal that same curious ghostlike sustained distress that made Lucie Höflich's performance so extraordinarily effective."

All in all, the performances of Pallenberg, Höflich, and Gülstorff, who played the father—"gloomy, tormented, wanting the good, producing ill, clumsy and slow-moving, revealing and then again concealing within himself deep feelings" (Kurt Pinthus)—were seen to be indisputably superior to those of the Italian actors. Only in the comparison between Marta Abba and the young Franziska Kinz, whose "nimble strength and clever trickery" (Paul Wiegler) had been highly praised by German critics, did Franz Servaes dare to make the observation that the "bold performance of the stepdaughter, played by the very gracious yet at the same time eminently modest Marta Abba," had sometimes the edge over their own Franziska Kinz.

The now-well-known Cherry Lane Theater, in Greenwich Village of New York City, opened in June 1948 with a production of this play. In the liberal newspaper *PM*, John S. Williams commented on their handling of the play:

> Possibly they have made a little too much of playing "6 Char." all over the theater. Practically all of the exits and entrances are made through the center aisle which leads to a good deal of twisting and turning among the audience and, in an intimate theater, brings the actors into such close proximity to the spectator that some of the illusion of reality is lost. On opening night, too, audience and players got all tangled up in the aisle at the opening of the second act. But these are rather trivial details in what is otherwise an auspicious beginning for this new group.

New and idiosyncratic is the interpretation given the play by Oscar Fritz Schuh in 1951 at the Kurfürstendamm Theater in Berlin. Schuh, like Reinhardt, takes the role of the director seriously. With this as a starting point he interprets the play anew. He does not see the director's world as an empty world of appearance but a field of work in which the fight for substance goes on just as it does in the performance of *Six Characters*. In this way the two groups balance themselves against each other. "They restore," wrote Walther Karsch, "the broken unity." The six characters and the actors make equal efforts to seize the play, which always eludes them.

That the play loses nothing of its effectiveness in this demythologized, more contemporary conception, can be seen from Friedrich Luft's enthusiasm. He speaks of a "glittering theatrical evening. . . . The dust had been swept from the boards. The stage became really a theater again. Something was happening. From the stage came challenge; and that blissful anxiety that always seizes hold of us when a genuine performance, a living, intelligent theatrical transformation, comes into being."

Of more recent German productions of *Six Characters*, that of Ulrich Erfurth (on 25 October 1953 in the theater of Düsseldorf) came closest to Pirandello's own conception. Here too the father and the stepdaughter are given prominence, the director and his actors confronting them are presented as easily caricatured professionals. Thus we get the sharp distinction: "On the one hand the actors plying their trade, on the other the Characters as agents of mankind, gripped by their destiny" (Otto Brües).

For Erfurth the drama lies here. The six characters, with all the violence of their destiny, are set against the triviality and insipidity of the actors:

> The father, as played by Richard Münch, is thrust by an infamous chance in the position of being a lover to his own stepdaughter, and this

gauchely lecherous provincial, with faltering limbs and tormented face, is driven to the theatrical director as hoped-for author. The daughter is Elisabeth Wiedemann—flashing with hatred, pale, edgy, hectic. She too is intent on the outcome as though heaven and earth depended on it. Then the mother, Gerda Maurus, burned out with pain, apathetic, until the shot rouses her to a cry of despair. [Gerhard Schön]

This exactly followed Pirandello's own conception of the dominance of the six characters. As he wrote in the foreword to the play, they find themselves in an "impossible situation from which they feel they must escape at whatever cost, as if it is a matter of life and death."

Tyrone Guthrie, as director and co-writer (with Michael Wager), took on the challenge of this difficult play in his 1955 production at the Phoenix Theater in New York City. Of this production John Beaufort, in the *Christian Science Monitor* (17 December 1955), wrote:

Tyrone Guthrie has bestowed his customary buoyant and inventive theatricalism on the most brilliant Phoenix production to date. Indeed, the puffs of smoke in which Madame Pace vanishes and the use of the dummy to simulate the body of the boy who commits suicide appear to be Guthrie innovations. No stage directions for such effects occur in the Dutton translation. They may—with justification—disturb Pirandello purists. The question as to whether the director has gone too far is certainly debatable.

But it cannot be denied that Mr. Guthrie gives the play a positive clarity. The definition is furthered in the bold colors of Alvin Colt's 1922 costumes for the rehearsing actors, contrasted with the mourning black of the Characters. It occurs in Klaus Holm's scenery and lighting. A clump of mundane stage ladders, for instance, casts a network of Feininger shadows on the backstage wall. Stage movement and grouping further enhance the defined effect. . . .

The performance ends, characteristically, with the repeated cry of "reality!" reverberating as if from some electronic echo chamber. An echo perhaps of Mr. Guthrie's days as a radio writer and director, it leaves an eerie impression.

The production of this play at the Martinique Theater in March 1963 was less controversial than that of Mr. Guthrie. The *New York Post* critic Richard Watts wrote approvingly (10 March 1963):

William Ball has staged it with imagination and without recourse to the farcical excess which I thought spoiled Tyrone Guthrie's version at the Phoenix a few years ago, and the Italian dramatist's famous fantasy examining the conflict between theatrical illusion and reality becomes as steadily absorbing as it is provocative.

Henry IV

CONTENTS: In the costume of Emperor Henry IV, who had been humiliated by Pope Gregory VII, a rich nobleman afflicted by jealousy and unrequited love plays the role of a madman. He lives in his country seat in Umbria, furnished and decorated in an exact imitation of the royal residence at Goslar. He is surrounded by courtiers dressed like German knights of the eleventh century. His madness, the result of an accident (more than twenty years before the time of the play his rival caused him to fall from his horse during a carnival procession), is long cured. But he deliberately continues to live in his illusionary world, cut off on all sides from reality.

The play begins shortly after the death of his sister, who had begged her son to do everything possible to free her brother once and for all from his madness. The nephew, the Marchese di Nolli, appears. With him he brings: a doctor, Dr. Genoni; the woman Henry IV had formerly loved, the Marchesa Matilda; her friend (Henry IV's rival), Baron Belcredi; and the marchesa's daughter, Frida, who is engaged to di Nolli.

The doctor suggests that a sharp jolt might cure Henry IV. He suggests that Frida, who resembles her mother to an extraordinary degree, show herself in the costume of the Marchesa of Tuscany. It was this costume her mother had worn at the time of the carnival, the costume in which she had had her portrait painted, the portrait Henry IV guards in his house like a relic.

By showing him the portrait come alive, side by side with the twenty-years-older mother, it is hoped that Henry IV's confused sense of time will be restored. But the opposite happens. Henry IV sees the plot for what it is, feels he is being made a fool of, and revenges himself by a brutal display of madness. He pretends to take Frida for the reality of his "dream" and embraces her. When Belcredi, who sees through the feigned madness, springs between them, Henry IV draws the sword of one of his councilors and stabs him.

Of the plays that made Pirandello famous, *Henry IV* is the most conventional in form. It was written in 1921, the same year *Six Characters* was premiered, but displays none of the dramatic devices of that play. Pirandello evidently found the correct dramatic form for *Henry IV* at the first attempt. This was not difficult, for the story underlying this play is comparatively simple, and at no point does it transcend the classical dramatic pattern. On the contrary, it so enriches it that life itself can be turned directly into theater, something that appeared impossible with *Six Characters*.

Henry IV is the typical eccentric who seeks refuge in a fiction because of a failed human relationship that humiliates him. He assumes an attitude of madness that makes right lie on his side. Thus he solves his conflict in the simplest way possible—by suppressing his personal past. The new assumed past then enables him to conceal his painful role of unhappy lover behind the more glittering and universally recognized role of the humiliated Henry IV.

The theater is exactly suited to such an exchange of roles. It provides all the means for creating a perfect illusion—costume, scenery, drama. And the catastrophe itself then follows as a necessary consequence of the confrontation with the other players who represent both the past and present reality—life itself that has been suppressed.

Thus we have a situation that can clearly be surveyed internally as well as externally. The tension lies entirely in the psychological, which is unlike what is normally thought of as real Pirandellian drama. Pirandello's psychology, like that of Strindberg, is permeated by the morbid. It has its rightful place right on the stage. In disguise, which is an indication of motivation, it can communicate itself and become comprehensible. Thus it is no longer—as is usual with Pirandello—an insoluble metaphysical secret.

The motivation is shown so clearly only because it is itself a theatrical stereotype. The story pattern that underlies this "historical" pseudotragedy is the usual triangular one of love, jealousy, and revenge—a Sicilian melodrama, as Eric Bentley called it, or, if you like, an opera libretto. Pirandello used the story only to provide a trauma for his protagonist. The theme itself did not interest him. He was interested only in the reaction to it of the character—the flight from humiliation into madness.

By contrast with *Six Characters*, who seek in vain for a role in which to lodge their trauma, the person of Henry IV disappears in the role. But the person also wants to get out of it. This is where the drama begins—at the point of crisis where the character wants to return from total illusion to reality and is given the possibility of doing so by external agents, the visits of the doctor, his former mistress, and his rival.

The encounter with the persons who were guilty of bringing about his original trauma unbalances the firmly established illusionary world of Henry IV. It begins to let in light, to take on a twilight existence. And only through this does life return and make the dramatic action possible.

The doctor feels he understands this instability. He decides that the picture of Henry IV's beloved, which hangs in the throne room as sign of his fixation, must come alive in Frida, dressed up for the part, and make possible the transition to truth.

Pirandello's usual tendency to let his plays explain themselves here becomes the whole principle that makes up the plot. Both sides see through the fiction and use it to further their own purposes. For the visitors it is a weapon against madness, for Henry IV an instrument of revenge.

In the great revelation scene in the second act, Henry IV admits the reasons for his playacting to one of his privy councilors. Because he cannot and will not conform, he forces the others to enter his world of illusion, making them into puppets. In this way he wins back the freedom of his own subjectivity. The others had earlier amused themselves at his expense. Now it is his turn to amuse himself at their expense. But at the same time he remains the prisoner of his self-chosen ceremonial. Because of the alienation of his past he cannot communicate himself, and his revenge remains a dumb one. His act of pretense seems to be fragmented within itself and is overburdened with diffuse emotions that seek relief in constantly new forms.

This division within himself gives rise to a drama of immense oppressiveness. His entrance, delayed over two lengthy introductory scenes, is frightening—and pompous. Flanked by two of his councilors who carry crown, scepter, and the globe with the cross, he enters the throne room in masklike dress.

He is "nearly fifty, very pale, gray-haired. But the hair on his temple and forehead is patently dyed blond, in a downright childish way. His face is tragically pale, his cheeks rouged. His eyes have a fixed stare. He bears himself with an affected humility. Over his kingly attire he wears the hairshirt as Henry IV wore at Canossa." Like his external appearance, his speech is ambiguous—at the same time very formal and spontaneous, declared commitment and affected declamation.

The guests, who appear before him in the dress of Henry IV's period, are his puppets, whom he lets dance on the strings of his caprice, taking their disguise seriously at one moment, seeing through it the next. He talks about the intrigues of the bishops, the slander against his holy mother Agnes. Then suddenly he breaks out of his role. Pointing to his dyed hair, he tells his former beloved that he does this for her sake.

It is no longer possible at this point to distinguish what is truth and what pretense—both are blurred. But even as he breaks out of his role, he is still acting. His naturalness is stylized; his pathos and his gestures those of a tragedian playing Hamlet. At the end of the scene Henry IV points "almost in fear" to his picture, which, together with that of his beloved, hangs in the throne room and depicts them in historical costume. For a moment there seems to become visible through his mask the real human being imprisoned in his fixation. But straightaway he disappears again in a terrifying pantomime of madness.

He notices his rival, Belcredi, who has come closer. To everyone's astonishment and horror, he runs to the throne, where his crown is lying, snatches it up, and hides it under his cowl. Then, after bowing several times with a crafty smile, he disappears.

This exaggerated reversion into madness reveals Henry IV's real sickness. He is no longer capable of articulating his position. At the approach of his rival, he backs into his world of illusion, which is the only place where he can be master of himself. For to acknowledge reality means, for him, to admit his defeat and expose to ridicule his own absurdity. He would be stripped. Thus, he retreats all the more violently into his disguise, which lends significance to his socially unrecognized introversion and frees him from the knowledge of his own banality.

The rejected metaphysical aspect here creeps back in again. Essentially, it is what makes Henry IV's love impossible. "One wasn't to toy with him," says the marchesa about her rejected lover. "There is nothing more funny. If men could only see themselves with this look of eternity in their eyes! It has always made me laugh so much."

Henry IV now projects this sense of the eternal, which the marchesa rejected.

Within the framework of the medieval order, which he as emperor represents, he makes his own feelings absolutely binding. They do not admit of any questioning. From this position he tyrannizes over his surroundings.

But he pays for his dominion with his "life." Because he cannot leave his imaginary world without losing his intoxicating sense of power, he attempts the opposite—to pull outside life forcibly into his illusion. When the stratagem with Frida in costume in the final scene is to give him back the "sense for the distance of time," he takes illusion for reality. He draws Frida to himself: "The dream has become alive with you. More alive than ever. Up there you were an image. Now you have been made a living person. You're mine. You're mine. I have a right to you."

But this time, too, it is Belcredi who opposes this fallacious claim. In all things, he is the opposite of Henry IV—sober and flexible, a champion of reality, who has never insisted on being taken seriously and thus won the woman he loved and acquired a natural authority. At this point he jumps at Henry IV and protests. Like the others, he has learned from the councilors that Henry IV only pretends to be mad. And for him the pretense has now come to an end. He is not in fancy dress, and he demands from Henry IV a statement of the truth. "You're not a madman."

In that same moment, when he is forced into a confrontation with reality, the feelings of revenge that Henry IV had nurtured for twenty years in the role he had assumed, break out of control. In a flash he draws the sword from the side of one of his councilors and drives it into Belcredi's body.

The deliberately provoked crisis does not take Henry IV out of his isolation. But it does, for the first time, reveal its real extent. The protest against his surroundings shows itself to be fatal, not only for the others but also for himself. Belcredi dies. And with his death Henry IV also destroys the possibility of a new life for himself, a life that recognizes the truth and is free from illusion. He has to go on playing the part of madman, to confirm the judgment of those around him, whom he had previously made game of, that he is a puppet, totally alienated, receiving his principles of action solely from without, from society.

More strongly than in his other plays Pirandello criticizes, with this conclusion, a mode of behavior that defends itself from the recognition of reality by the illusion of a closed system. The seemingly eccentric case of Henry IV becomes a general pattern of alienation, of the isolation from life brought about by adherence to ideologies, by the dictates of society, by illusion-making, and by the pathos of introversion. With almost clinical exactness Pirandello showed how society's system of coercion brings about the disintegration of the personality, which moves from deliberate madness to instinct-driven, uncontrollable crime.

Possessing these traits, the figure of Henry IV seems like a conjuration of the fascist phenomenon. The portagonist's behavior exemplifies the sickness of a society that found its expression in the dictatorship of Mussolini at the very time that Pirandello wrote this play.

Pirandello saw these connections very clearsightedly. He criticized the power complex as irrational impulse, as illusionary superstructure to a psychic defect. He demythologized the "hero," whom he put into a drama that is a parody of both a tragedy and a historical play. He constructed what looks like a powerful personality but reveals itself as one lacking in awareness and being dominated by a mechanical dependence on the subconscious and the demands of the environment.

But despite all critical detachment, Pirandello loved his protagonist. And this too alludes to his later ambivalent attitude to fascism. Henry IV is shown not as a bugaboo but as a monster who towers over the others in grandeur, power, and self-sufficiency. There is around him an aura of a deeper, more general justification, the melancholy fascination of suffering that is the symptom of a basically nihilistic devaluation of values.

For Pirandello, Henry IV expresses the spirit of his period with more awareness than do his opponents. This gives him a kind of superiority. He knows that his costume is the "obvious and freely chosen ridiculous distortion of that endless masquerade, which dupes and enslaves us when we disguise ourselves as what we believe ourselves to be—without knowing it."

"Life is one huge puppet show." This was Piran-

dello's view even when he was only nineteen. It was a
favorite formula that he repeated with constantly new
variations. When Henry IV speaks like this, it is Pirandello speaking through him. Pirandello did of course
criticize the ensuing act of murder. But it also provided him with his argument: that in a world without
context and meaning, the need for self-realization
leads of necessity to violence.

Thus by the detour of unmasking, Henry IV arrives
at a new mythos. In his wrong he is right—because
circumstances want it so. That circumstances too can
be changed remains outside his experience. That is
why the end changes nothing. It only comes back all
the more strongly to its point of departure. His life
remains without a future, a stagnating self-enclosed
vision of chaos and emptiness.

Henry IV was premiered in 1922 in Milan. The day
after Pirandello's company had performed *Six Characters* in Berlin in October 1925, they played *Henry IV*.
This time the impact was different. On the whole it
was acknowledged that the play was an "undoubted
theatrical success." Critical opinion was satisfied and
asserted that the theatrical parry and thrust had come
off well.

But most of all the vital, completely unmannered
performance of Lamberto Picasso was this time completely convincing in the role of Henry IV. Picasso
did not allow himself to be tempted merely to play at
being disguised. Instead he felt his disguise in all its
weaknesses with so personal a vitality that it became
immediately credible. "Picasso's Enrico," wrote Julius
Knopf, "does not perform tragedy, he is it."

Picasso held them by the unsentimental modulations of his harsh voice, and the "gripping" double play of madness and resignation. At the same time, however, he also showed his awareness of the part he was playing, the disguise was seen through. In this way the tragedy acquired greater relativity, the histrionic element broke through and absorbed the heavily pregnant dialogue.

It was not, however, until Alexander Moissi played the part that the play became a theatrical event. This performance took place shortly afterward at the Tribune in Berlin, Viktor Barnowsky's theater. Moissi gave greater depth to the figure of Henry IV, Germanized it and gave it a "Hamlet-like glitter." What he communicated was above all suffering—a contorted, ritualized pain that was intended to move the audience deeply.

Moissi eschewed noisiness, eruptive scenes, hysteria. His performance was "still, concentrated, and totally subservient to the role." It was this that gave it a subtle provocativeness. With sublime mimic art, stylized talk, and dramatically calculated movements, he projected the state of a "soul charged with a task to which it does not feel itself equal," and communicated the suppressed fear, despair, and malice of Henry IV. "The courtly constraint of his sham king seems a bitter irony, the piercing eyes look deep into the helplessness of his involuntary fellow actors, the watchful sharpness of his observation tears the masks from their faces" (Alfred Klaar).

The impression was powerful, spellbinding. Moissi dominated the stage. His art, it was said, was superior to Pirandello's stratagems. "Alongside the emotions that flowed from him and took hold of the spectators, the playwright's pseudo-art, his mirage paled into nothingness" (Felix Hollaender).

Henry IV is above all a vehicle of a single role, "a primordial part of the acting art," as Albert Schulze Vellinghausen wrote. That is why it has always tempted the great mimic actors. In addition to Moissi, Georges Pitoëff, Jean Vilar, and Gustaf Gründgens played the part with outstanding success. Pitoëff played it as if Henry IV were a grotesque puppet. He wore exaggerated make-up, which was drastically changed at different points. At times he trembled with excitement when the external world impinged on him; then again he was completely rigid, when he returned to his own inner isolation.

For Gründgens, who produced the play in 1951 in a taut setting, the role demanded, above all, a constant shifting, a Pirandellian alternation between madness and reality, irony and despair. "So ingeniously did Gründgens balance on the frontier between real illusion and acted reality that the boundary was completely blotted out for the spectator" (Heinz Liepman). The beginning was almost "devilishly comical." But it did not remain "fixed in the attempt to create a pathological study" (Vielhaber). "What we experience is the great battle between two spirits—the clear-sighted man of irony, and the lonely man of despair" (Vielhaber). What we see, wrote Erich Franzen, "are breath-taking transitions from the hidden ironies of the misanthrope to the suffocating pain under his own freely-unfreely worn mask."

In the *New York Times* (7 February 1968) Clive Barnes started his review of a new production of *Henry IV* with the following words:

> Luigi Pirandello, with his strange thoughts of illusion and reality, his tortured concept of schizoid man, his constant antithetical equation between order and freedom, is the playwright for our times. Born just more than a century ago —there were few celebrations—Pirandello, more even than the later Beckett, Genet or Ionesco, has laid on the shaking line what we, here and now, are about. There is a mask, so Pirandello says, and there is a face. Choose, my friends by all means, but do not imagine for a moment that too much depends upon your choice. We live in a world divided, and the division is larger in ourselves. . . . These thoughts on Pirandello have been prompted by the current production of Pirandello's "Henry IV" by the Yale School of Drama Repertory Theater. Henry is not perhaps Pirandello's greatest character, but he is indisputably his greatest metaphor.

This production was staged by Carl Weber, who used Eric Bentley's translation. As for the acting of Kenneth Haigh, Mr. Barnes wrote:

> As Henry IV, his cheeks grotesquely rouged as Pirandello insisted, his movements puppet-oriented, his eyes staring blankly into the grossly insensitive world of another reality, Kenneth Haigh is fantastic. With this zombie-like understanding of a world of blood-struck illusion, Mr. Haigh makes his case for being regarded as one

of the finest actors of the English-speaking theater. I have seen him in many roles, but in nothing
else has he burned his way into my memory.

One interesting recent performance was that offered
at the Citizens' Theater in Glasgow, in which Albert
Finney delivered a remarkable performance. In an
eloquent review Kenneth Tynan wrote:

> . . . the thrust of his temperament . . . carries him
> to hard-won triumph. His very presence, relaxed
> and watchful, the long arms dangling, the heavy
> head balefully swaying in search of opposition,
> imparts a sense of danger that is authentically
> feudal; and as he lopes crabwise around the stage,
> we are unnerved by the knowledge that at any
> moment he may do something violent and un-
> predictable.
>
> This ability to arouse in one's audience the
> expectation of being astounded is not only car-
> dinal to Henry; it is a hallmark of first-rate
> acting. I shall not quickly forget the fumbling
> convulsion of disgust—a sort of manual regurgi-
> tation—with which Mr. Finney discards the
> sword he has just used to impale the hated lover.
> As for his voice, it is always pungent and fre-
> quently thrilling. Only a handful of living actors
> can make a whole audience gasp and recoil with
> a single syllable, and one of these is Mr. Finney.

The most recent example of the desire of great
actors to play this oversize role is Rex Harrison. His
performance as Henry IV opened at New York City's
Ethel Barrymore Theater on 28 March 1973, follow-

ing a lengthy pre-Broadway tour. Starring with Harrison was the brilliant Eileen Herlie, as the Marchesa Matilda. In the *New York Times* (8 April 1973) Walter Kerr praised Harrison's ability to portray Henry's vacillations between his roles of madman and sane man:

> Mr. Harrison . . . is at his very best in this turnabout. From emotional displays that are mere posturing he is able to turn to a cackling, quizzical directness, to release the lightly sardonic inflections that go so well with the wickedly amused glint in his eye. Playful, he is immensely entertaining; serious, as he contemplates the real world to which he may return and asks, "Is it so different out there?" he is genuinely reflective. A mind begins to display its shape behind what has been a busy, a merely busy, façade.

Clive Barnes (in his earlier review in the *New York Times*), however, considered the madness of Harrison's Henry to be "tumultous rather than introspective" and the character himself "almost compulsively tragic" with "too little humor to him." The gloomy scenery —"more like impoverished Shakespeare than elaborate Pirandello"—and the directing by Clifford Williams were also attacked by Mr. Barnes for having too little sense of fantasy to them.

Nevertheless, both critics agreed that the production was a near necessity for serious theatergoers. For, as Mr. Kerr asserted:

> The internal argument of "Henry IV" is not especially profound when we get to it. Every

last man of us, adopting a role in life, wears the mask of that role. . . .

But if we have played this game before, and if some of its terms seem commonplace enough now, we are still held to it by the magnet of an intelligence, a force felt even while we are faulting the craftmanship. Pirandello's is almost an obsessed intelligence, a concentration so intense that we are given no choice but to attend—there are no openings in the landscape through which we may slip away.

To Clothe the Naked

CONTENTS: Central to the story is the moving experience of Ersilia Drei, a young governess aged twenty. She had been dismissed without notice by her employers, Consul Grotti of Smyrna and his wife, because of an accident that brought about the death of the child in her charge. She arrives in Rome without money and has another disappointment there. She discovers that the man who promised her marriage in Smyrna is shortly to be married to another woman. In a moment of irresolution and self-humiliation, she gives herself to the first stranger she meets on the street. Then she goes into the park and takes poison. She is rescued. With this the play begins.

The interest of the press in her circumstances leads to a wave of curiosity and sentimentality among the public. Ludovico Nota, a well-known writer, is moved by the story and takes Ersilia into his house in order to use her as the heroine of a novel or play. But Ersilia cannot get away from her past. Franco Laspiga, the fiancé, and Grotti, the consul, force their way into Nota's house and destroy Nota's preconceptions about the event.

Ersilia now falls victim to ever new explanations. The fiancé Laspiga is obsessed by the need to put everything right. The consul Grotti contradicts the newspaper account, according to which Ersilia had given as her motive for suicide her disappointment at her fiancé's betrayal. He accuses her of being a murderer. We are told that he had been Ersilia's lover and that the child had fallen from the terrace while they were in each others' arms.

Nota, at first made angry by these contradictory accounts, finally comes to see the story with new eyes. It turns for him into the comedy of a lie exposed.

Ersilia, on the other hand, is destroyed by the three men's attempts to turn her into an object of their imagination. She, who had been lying in order to acquire a beautiful dress to die in, as she describes it, sees through the lies of the others, who, to justify themselves, thrust roles on her in which she does not recognize herself.

She wants truth, but truth proves itself to be fluid, continually changing in the encounter with others. It is only in death that she manages to show herself as she really is. She takes poison for the second time in order to die without lies because she cannot any longer live with lies.

To Clothe the Naked is a direct successor to *Six Characters*, even though it was written in 1922, after *Henry IV*. Pirandello seems to have done for Ersilia what he could not do for the stepdaughter in *Six*

Characters. In Ersilia he returns to the original story and completes it. But the result is dubious, precisely because it tries to leave no questions unanswered. The unambiguousness and straightforwardness of the story that Pirandello tried to reconstruct makes it even more obvious than *Six Characters* did, however useless the old dramatic concepts are for Pirandello's new ideas.

In *To Clothe the Naked* there is no sign of the critical, reflective self-awareness that played so disturbing and illuminating a part in the construction of *Six Characters*. It disappears in the story of the principal character. This time Pirandello will do nothing to minimize its force. Ersilia, sentimental figure of a magazine story, turns in the course of the play into a tragic heroine, whose pathetic fate it is to demonstrate by her death the insolubility of the problem of identity.

The curtain falls, in the classical manner, after the triumphant song of the dying woman, who transfigures her death by vindicating it. No doubt remains, no Pirandellian laughter. Death gives the simple answer to a difficult problem. It teaches that he who wants to free himself from the entanglements with social lies and self-deception, he who seeks nothing save the truth—and himself—must die.

One almost has the impression that Pirandello, in making these simplifications, acted blindly against himself, suppressing all his objections only in order to help his protagonist achieve her theatrical objectives. As in *Six Characters*, he sets against the raw material of the drama presented by a character, the formative, re-creating principle of art, represented this time by the figure of a writer. In the role of Ludovico

Nota, who takes Ersilia into his house, not merely because he discovers in her life the seeds of a story or novel but also in order to begin a new life with her, lies the essential pivot of the play.

We surely have the right to assume that the figure of Nota is a self-portrait of Pirandello himself: "He is level-headed and weighs everything carefully. He lacks the gift of easily evoking sympathy and trust. As he is not successful in simulating any kind of warmth, he tries, at least, to appear amiable. But this amiability often disturbs and confuses more than it endears."

The lack of natural contact and its artificial exaggeration, which Pirandello observed in himself, are for him typical characteristics of the writer. Nota is alienated from life, but at the same time all the greedier for it. This makes for problems in his relationship with Ersilia from the start.

When Ersilia appears, Nota already has the complete idea for the novel ". . . All the situations and individual details . . . wonderful! The Orient . . . the little villa on the sea with its terrace . . . you there as governess . . . the child that falls from the balcony . . . your dismissal . . . the trip, your arrival here . . . the sad surprise . . . all this, all this, without having seen you. Without knowing you." Nota intends not only to write this novel, but to live its continuation, with Ersilia. The writing of it is to give his life a new immediacy.

Ersilia's story at first develops, like that of *Six Characters*, from opposition to the formalizing and greedy demands of art. She too is a person in search of an author. She comes to Nota hoping that her miserable life with all its wretchedness, its sad failures and sufferings, might at least serve as material for a novel. She has too much of what Nota lacks. She wants to get rid of the burden of life, to know it has been absorbed into the beautiful tidiness of a novel.

But she does not see herself in Nota's story. She wants to be depicted as the person she really is, not the one someone else has invented. But her struggle for self-assertion remains weak, if only because this time the demands of art also remain weak. Nota moves further and further into the background, turning into a fringe character who lets himself be displaced by Ersilia, who still drags around with her the life she cannot overcome.

The theme life and art, at first introduced with some effectiveness, cannot seem to develop the required dramatic impetus. Nota's function is confined to helpless watching and trivial comments. Unless of course one regards the scene of the action (which all takes place in Nota's room) as an indication that the whole story is simply an idea in the dramatist's mind.

It is true that the encounters of Ersilia with the fiancé and the consul seem like attempts to provide her with a motivation, to "interpret" her character. And the failure seems to repeat the conflict between matter and form. But the level of meaning remains unclear. Everything—the course of the story, the nature of the parts, the awareness of the characters—lies on the surface, even though it everywhere tries to burst out of its narrow framework. It lacks any other perspective save that of the theater of illusion.

This enables the play itself to develop all the more effectively. Ersilia can say all that is in her, can act out her despair—to the full. But she lacks, by contrast with the Six Characters and Henry IV, the perspective of self-awareness, and thus her explanation, powerfully as it is worded, remains mired in clichés.

She resists the hypotheses that Nota, Laspiga, and Grotti offer her. But her only answer is an unreflected, sentimental feeling of her own nothingness ("I have never had the strength to be anything") and of self-pity ("I was lying on the street, denuded of everything"). It is the weakness of the protagonist, motivated as she is, that she cannot get beyond this point or raise any other questions. And the weakness of the play as a whole is that every argument seeking to explore the background ends in the same vague sentimental inability to escape from determinism.

What sets the story moving even before the actual play begins is a dreamlike experience. This is the eastern night, in which Laspiga, on a visit to Smyrna, promises marriage to Ersilia: an ecstatic, enchanted moment in which, as Laspiga says, the "soul . . . breathes so redeemed and liberated . . . in a different, more glowing ambience, where even the most difficult things become quite easy."

It is this certain moment of enchantment that happens to almost all Pirandellian protagonists, who become its victims. Something lightninglike breaks into the person, some element of nature very different from anything found in society, and alters the person's entire pattern of behavior. When this happens to the person, his life orientation reverts to the primitive. It is reduced into pure instinct that reacts with blind necessity against the mechanics of convention. Thus, a dangerous process of social disintegration is initiated.

In *To Clothe the Naked* one intoxicating moment releases a chain of catastrophes that culminate in Ersilia's death. The meeting with Laspiga has a far-reaching effect. He leaves Smyrna after having aroused Ersilia. Thus, her unconscious sensuality transfers itself to Grotti, who seduces her. Both fall into a frenzy of passion that leads to oblivion. During yet another moment of passion, they fail to notice the child, who falls from the terrace and dies.

There is a clear resemblance here to the theme of *Six Characters*. Here also instinct kills life that is dependent on a stable social order. But in *Six Characters* the logical sequence of events was interrupted by continued uncertainty about a theme that reflected nothing save the coarsened pattern of bourgeois morality. What came through was only a fear that could not be reasoned away.

Here, on the contrary, where Ersilia is given the opportunity fully to formulate her experiences, we are once again shown Pirandello's fixation on an ideologically simplified plan of action. The complex social interconnections reduce themselves to a simple contrast in which instinct and convention confront each other in a straight polarity. The play runs its appointed course without any pointed countermoves.

The appearance of Laspiga and Grotti only hastens the destruction to which Ersilia has been fated from the beginning. Even when she first appears, she is already in a state of diminished vitality. Externally she still shows signs of integration to a social order: "She wears a simple blue, rather faded dress, like young teachers and governesses habitually wear." But her face already shows the marks of death. "She has just escaped death and thus is very pale. There is a lost look in her shadowed eye caverns."

Her desire, once released, has destroyed her; it has driven her from Laspiga to Grotti, from Grotti onto the streets. She has become the helpless victim of circumstances arising out of that one magical moment, without attempting to form any concept of protest, save to seek refuge in death. But this too is nothing but a conventionally dictated gesture, like the attempts of Laspiga and Grotti socially to integrate the moment of passion. Laspiga does it by creating a moral obligation from out of the "dreamlike experience" in order to "make up for everything." Grotti does it by accepting the condemnation of society with despair, confirming Ersilia's guilt as murderess, but in a kind of masochism wanting to remain in it with her: "I need you, I want you . . . we are both unhappy."

The scene between Grotti and Ersilia is the high point of the drama. Here the story acquires an impressive power of conviction, because it points out, and casts doubt on, its own clichés. At first Ersilia appears exactly as Grotti wishes to portray her. She becomes the object of his fury, his reproaches at her for having lied. Why did she not tell the press that she wanted to kill herself not on account of her dismissal and Laspiga's broken promise but because of her own feelings of guilt? But in the course of these recriminations she more and more discards the role that Grotti has created for her. She appears to emancipate herself, takes an equally furious position, and throws Grotti's accusations back at him:

ERSILIA: You grabbed when I was still so wholly aroused by him and could no longer resist. Just deny I bit and scratched you.

GROTTI: You cheap little tramp! It was you who led me on.

ERSILIA: That's not true. It just isn't true. Never. It was you.

GROTTI: In the beginning perhaps. But afterward?

ERSILIA: Never! Never!

GROTTI: You took my arm secretly!

ERSILIA: That's a lie!

GROTTI: A lie? You're the liar. You even stuck a needle in my shoulder once.

ERSILIA: Because you didn't leave me in peace, sir.

GROTTI: Just listen to her! Suddenly she's calling me sir!

ERSILIA: I was your employee.

GROTTI: And that's why you did what I wanted?

ERSILIA: My body did it, not my heart. I felt only hatred.

GROTTI: But it also gave you pleasure!

These are, to the very wording, formulas provided by society as seeming explanations of such a situation. In the excited exchange, in the simplifications and pathetic overstressed formulas ("It also gave you pleasure!" "My body did it, not my heart"), subliminal emotions gleam through, which, however, cannot come to expression.

Both characters, Ersilia and Grotti, act out the scene in order to present themselves to one another in a certain light. But they are not sure that they can express what is in them. Thus they leap from one excuse to the next. There are sudden outbursts, a series of exaggerated gestures. They feel "depressed, close to fainting, as if they were crazy," etc.

Passion has no conventional forms but remains masked, imprisoned by society's taboos. Disguised as compassion, it still tries to break out in Grotti at the end: "You are still more desperate than I . . . and how changed you are . . . how pitiful you look [goes toward her, wants to take her in his arms], Ersilia." But this time she sees through the deception. She pushes Grotti away, runs to the window, and opens it. "I'm going to scream!" She wants to break out of the vicious circle of illusion, determined to expose every new lie and also her earlier one.

Ersilia's attitude at the end of the play, when she is preparing for death, no longer achieves this process of dramatization and recognition, schizoid as it is and working its way through all dissimulations. At this point the play once again sinks into a flat obviousness of meaning. The language of this final mood of exaltation has the same masklike pathos that emerges in the Grotti scene.

> "Yes, another handful of filth, so that I am wholly sunk in the mire—God, how loathsome! How disgusting! And I wanted to get at least a decent dress through death. Do you now see why I lied? Only for this reason, I swear it! In all my life I never managed to get a decent dress. One in which I could have looked like something, one that the dogs would not have torn from my body—the many dogs that have always and everywhere hunted me. . . ."

But this time the cliché is not contradicted. Ersilia perishes in her sentimental self-interpretation. Thus, right remains on her side, at least within the play. That this death too is only a "beautiful dress" is made quite clear, but merely by way of a necessary summing up that excludes all further discussion.

In September 1950 this infrequently produced play was offered, under the title *Naked*, by the Provincetown Playhouse. It did not evoke enthusiasm in Brooks Atkinson, who wrote (*New York Times*, 7 September 1950):

> Under Frank Corsaro's direction the performance is at least animated and irrelevantly amusing at times. Mercedes Shirley, Anne Shropshire, Rudolph Weiss and Bernard Kates give an impression of being competent actors. If they had something substantial to work with, they probably could make a play out of it. "Naked" is not so much profound as poorly written, and no actor can do much for it today.

Each in His Own Way

CONTENTS: "This play should begin in the street or, better, in the square in front of the theater," wrote Pirandello in the introduction to *Each in His Own Way*. Newspaper sellers are shouting out the headlines of a special edition: "The suicide of the painter La Vela, and today's performance in [the name of the theater in which performance is being given]." This newspaper report, or rather its subsequent effects, provide the theme of the play.

La Vela had surprised his fiancée, the actress Amelia Moreno, with his sister's fiancé, Baron Nuti, and thereupon shot himself. Since then Amelia and Nuti have been social outcasts. Becoming the talk of the drawing rooms, this scandal continued to evoke new opinions and counteropinions, creating factions and destroying friendships.

In two acts Pirandello described what happened as a result of these differing views. Two friends, Doro Palegari and Francesco Savio, young men of the highest society, came to disagree violently during a discussion of the Moreno case. (In the play this character is called Delia Morello.) Doro had defended Delia against Francesco, but this causes him to be suspected of being in love with her. To correct this impression, he takes the opposite view the next evening and seriously offends Francesco, who has come around to thinking his friend was right after all. A duel seems inevitable.

Shortly afterward, however, Delia Morello arrives to thank Doro for having sided with her and so confirming her self-justification. This makes Doro return to his own earlier opinion. But he wavers yet again when he tells Delia of Francesco's objections. She suddenly admits that Francesco could be right too.

The second act is a repetition of an opinion changed, but this time it occurs in Francesco. The act begins with Francesco's preparations for the duel. Then Delia Morello appears, and under the influence of her visit he gives up his intention of dueling. But at the same time Delia's lover, Michele Rocca (alias Baron Nuti), rushes in, in order to thank Francesco on his own behalf for defending him against Doro.

But as soon as he sees Delia, they both recognize the truth—their passion for each other. They forget the others, fall into each other's arms, and Rocca carries her away with him. There is no third act. The interludes that Pirandello places after the first and second acts, and in which he continues the argument as critic of the performance, with the help of an imaginary theater audience, serve to analyze the play. The scandal repeats itself here too. In the audience as spectators are Amelia Moreno and Baron Nuti, the real protagonists of the play that reproduced their story, so they say, in a distorted way.

After the second act Amelia Moreno runs indignantly onto the stage and slaps the actress who plays Delia Morello. But when she comes unexpectedly upon Nuti, the two repeat the scene that they have just seen and criticized on the stage. They rush at each other and both disappear. The confusion among actors and audience is complete. The actors refuse to go on, and the audience becomes hysterical. The manager has finally to come to the front of the stage and cancel the performance.

In *Six Characters* Pirandello came upon the real problem of his own and of the contemporary drama for the first time, and apparently by chance. He had openly questioned the validity of the theater as audiences knew it, with its traditional roles, themes, and techniques. He had demonstrated its uselessness as a medium for creating self-awareness. With this extreme of self-criticism, the end of all drama seemed to have been reached, allowing of no further development. And in the next two years Pirandello did indeed begin to revert to the more conventional pattern of playmaking.

With *Each in His Own Way*, however, Pirandello suddenly took up the theater's conflict with itself again and drove it in a still more radical, more deliberate way, to the final phase of its paralysis. He turned the play-within-the-play technique into a virtuoso means to push the drama out of itself and let it transcend not only its own fictitious but its actual limits.

Pirandello left the stage, climbed across the footlights into the street, and mingled with life, with the spectators. The ultimate result of this theater within the theater is the abolition of all distance between stage and audience. The audience turns into actors, the production into total improvisation, theater into reality, reality into theater, as in *Tonight We Improvise*, which is the final play in the *teatro-sul-teatro* trilogy, into which Pirandello grouped the three plays *Six Characters in Search of an Author*, *Each in His Own Way*, and *Tonight We Improvise*.

The disintegration of the traditional theater results, however, as in *Six Characters*, in a theater plus. The levels of meaning multiply and extend to a point at which everything, even what was originally outside the theater, is brought within the limits of the play. The stimulus for this dilation is in every case the inability of the theater meaningfully to present a dramatic theme.

In *Each in His Own Way*, too, there exists in the center of the play an emotional impulse that seeks in vain for a definitive expression, leaping from level to level of meaning and finally driving not only the actors but also the audience "out of themselves." Around this innermost play within the play, the scandalous affair of Delia Morello and Michele Rocca, there rotate all the other levels in ever widening perspectives: society discussing the further scandal between Doro Palegari and Francesco Savio; the fictitious public and the real protagonists, Amelia Moreno and Baron Nuti; and finally the actual public that already heard the story outside the theater through the cries about a special news edition and the appearance of the actress impersonating Amelia Moreno and the actor playing

Baron Nuti. Both were seen to be in a state of great excitement at the box office and in the foyer of the theater—a living commentary to the play.

Within these different levels there is repeated the search for motive, for the meaning of the events and the play. The drama of jealousy that lies in the Delia-Michele scenes is no longer seen as continuous action but only as remnants of an abrupt attempt to reconstruct the persona of a character at odds with herself and with society. Since the infidelity that drove her fiancé to suicide, Delia has lost the awareness of her own identity. Society sees her only as the embodiment of wickedness and madness, and she herself has nothing to oppose this with save the presentation of a rouged and powdered emptiness. She no longer understands herself and thus cannot make herself comprehensible to others. Her face has become a mask that expresses nothing save a rigid state of having been subdued by something alien.

Delia seeks to escape from this distorted existence into a new role. When she appears before Doro, she seems to recognize herself again in his opinion of her: "It is as if you have lived my life to its core . . . but understanding me in a way I never—never understood myself."

Doro offers Delia a motive that seems to fit—that she got involved with Michele only to stop her fiancé from making a marriage that would have been a disaster for him. But this too is a mask that becomes askew as soon as Doro tells her that in Francesco's eyes her act was all part of an insidious game to blackmail her fiancé and drive him to despair. Suddenly Delia covers her face with her hands and admits that this too could have been true. It is a gesture Pirandello frequently employs to show a person's inability to relate in interpersonal relations. When Delia accepts both views as possibilities they seem to glide off from her. She cannot come to any understanding of what really happened and is left once more in mute isolation.

Nevertheless, the end of this small residual drama, a short scene at the conclusion of the second act, seems to indicate the true reasons for the liaison. Delia and Michele meet for the first time since the scandalous event. They had previously renounced each other, abused and demeaned each other in the sight of society. When they meet again, each relinquishes his assumed position. Delia, as Pirandello writes in the stage directions, "suddenly feels how the lie falls away from her, the lie with which she had armed herself as defense against the secret passion which, from their first meeting, had violently attracted them toward each other."

Their passion erupts as a suppressed monstrously intensified compulsion in a love-hate relationship that drives them apart and then again toward each other. They are like "two wild animals," say the others in disgust. But in their wild madness Michele and Delia discover the truth. " 'You wanted me like I wanted you, from the moment we first saw each other,' " Michele proclaims. Delia "dashes to him like a flame, thrusting aside the two men who are restraining him. 'Yes, it's true! It's true!' "

This then is the moment of truth. But what does it look like? The recognition scene is loud, turbulent, theatrical. The dialogue is one long stammering, groaning, screaming. A frantic tumult is staged. In an ecstatic exchange, the characters move toward and away from each other until the obsessed pair passionately embrace, and he carries her into the garden.

As always in a Pirandello drama, when the action gets near the truth, it appears in a guise of exaggerated illusion. The final unmasking presents itself as the most strident mask. The theatrical convention is overemphasized in order to demonstrate its uselessness. What happens to the characters no longer fits into the dramatic mold. It spills out of it and pervades the forms and gestures with emotions that can clearly be seen as theatrical. The dramatic elements reveal themselves as a brittle, chaotic mask from which escapes life and therefore truth.

Up to this point the play follows the course of a typically Pirandellian drama. The story of an individual case is acted out to such excess that it leads to an ad absurdum and cryptically points to a more general disturbance.

What is new in *Each in His Own Way* is that the process of disintegration, which the character reveals as his individual drama, is shown in the play itself as a deficiency of general consciousness. Society no longer confronts the character as a rigid homogeneous entity but shows itself as an unstable group of people, each of whom suffers from the same deficiency.

The drawing-room setting in which the events take place already points to the split of society. The first act takes place in an ancient patrician Italian palace. In the background can be seen a sumptuous drawing room, brightly lit and filled with an animated group. In the foreground, however, less brightly lit, there is a small room that one of the guests calls the "confessional chapel." Here, in this twilight sphere, away from society's glittering exterior, the increasingly insecure, disturbed inner situation develops.

The guests come in twos and threes out of the brightly lighted drawing room to the small room in the front and confide to one another that they can no longer communicate with one another.

Pirandello deliberately gave no names to the characters who appear at the beginning of the play. They are stock characters—the Young Man, the Old Man, the First Young Lady, the Second Young Lady. Their talk is purely stereotyped, paradigmatic, a mere replica of a certain manner of thinking and feeling.

Apropos of the scandalous affair, the Young Man and the Old Man come to the conclusion, after a rigorously logical, Socratic dialogue, that there can be no objective verdict—that no man can have an opinion binding on others since every man can only have his own subjective view that can be contradicted or seen differently by the next man.

In the conversation between the First Young Lady and the Second Young Lady we catch a glimpse of the disorientation in a person split within by passion. The First Young Lady says: "But what am I, actually? I'm sure I don't know. I assure you I don't know— even myself! Everything is in movement, intangible, weightless."

There is one character in the play who gives a special meaning to these generalized statements of a deep though only mechanical anxiety—Diego Cinci. Diego, like Laudisi in *Thus It Is (If It Seems So to You)*, is the type of man who loves to reason. He is himself untouched by events and therefore has a sharper and clearer understanding of their deeper causes.

He is the center of reflection in the play, and in the light of this function, an epic character who demonstrates that the experience that the play tries to analyze totally defies presentation as theater.

When he, Doro's friend, is pressed more and more hysterically by Doro's mother out of her fear that Doro is in love with Delia Morello, he is suddenly evasive. In light conversational tone he asks her if she can imagine "a carriage . . . on a sunny afternoon in summertime." And as she looks at him dumbfounded, unable to understand, he tells her, seriously and with deep feeling, about his mother's death. He had failed to notice she was dying because he was at that moment completely engrossed with watching the blind, Sisyphean effort of an insect trying unsuccessfully to escape from a glass of water.

With this apparent stratagem Diego wards off the intense emotion long since overcome. He has lost those feelings regulated by society, those feelings that make a scandal possible, because of his bewilderment over the absurdity of life. While around him there take place the great human dramas, he is immersed in his observation of the small and meaningless ones. He no longer has any feeling for the immense drama of man's existence. But because of this lack he has an all the more subtle sensitivity for chance events, for trifles, for sudden changes in reaction.

His mother's last moments go unnoticed because he is at the time absorbed in an insignificant object. It was not only the insect that obtruded itself on him, as he later explains to Doro but also the white majolica cup on the highboy with a single blue line around it. And then: "The chiming of the clock! Ding! Dong! Ding! Dong! Eight . . . nine. I counted them all. . . . Ten . . . eleven. . . . The chiming of the wall clock. Twelve! Then you wait for the chiming every quarter hour." Tiredness had deprived him of his sense of continuity, had delivered him over to unconscious feelings that were reflected in his face as "a sort of happy fright" when his mother's gasping stops for a moment.

Diego explains this inability to behave in the socially expected manner as shock. Similar descriptions, but only outside the theater, are found in Gottfried Benn, Sartre, and Camus. But this shock no longer has anything dramatic about it in the ordinary sense.

Diego, it is true, is still far removed from the composure of Camus's "stranger," who, having already adapted himself to the experience of the absurd, is not inhibited from falling asleep or lighting a cigarette in the mortuary beside the bier on which his mother is lying. Diego, however, though he has already abandoned the broad conventions of life that are characteristic of bourgeois drama, is still alarmed at not being able to react in the normal manner. But at the same time he accepts this lack of response as a symptom of his changed awareness and begins to practice registering the new.

In a play that is so patently concerned with more and more theatricality, a character such as Diego, with its antidramatic perspectives, seems at first to be completely alien. But, actually, it only expresses more explicitly the antidramatic tendencies that histrionics bring out in Pirandello. In the totality of the play

Diego expresses those aspects of the Pirandellian experience that will no longer present themselves in a compact form but diverge into many different directions. Alienation is presented in all its different forms —in exaggerated melodrama, pseudological dialogue, in mechanical exchange of opinion.

But Diego also retains a hidden dramatic function. Wherever he appears, his assertions, made from a position of noninvolvement, put the drama in perspective and provoke challenge. He arouses anger and everywhere excites society's easily stimulated hysteria. This makes him into a voice of Pirandello himself. Like Pirandello, he casts doubt on the dramatic value of the story, thereby arousing an excitement in the audience—a reaction that resembles a response to drama but is nothing save the unarticulated expression of a complete loss of orientation.

"I am not looking for agreement," said Pirandello in an interview about *Each in His Own Way*:

> Discussion is the success I welcome most. I want to arouse people. To be simply accepted by them without argument would be humiliating. Discussion and disagreement are valuable and necessary. Just when a work of art is moving in a new direction and is therefore full of vitality, it must be able to arouse differences of opinion, and agreement, in order to make room for various contrary opinions.

Granting that the exchange of views will lead to a fruitful result, this sounds like a sensible and democratic approach. But in fact Pirandello was concealing his real intention from the press, and perhaps from himself. He wanted to arouse the public, it is true. He wanted discussion, excitement. But he wanted this only in order to pull the ground from under society's feet.

With all his horror at destructiveness, there also lurked in Pirandello a tendency to take pleasure in anarchy. Diego feels jubilant when he sees the collapse of all those artificial forms that our dull daily life has solidified.

Pirandello wanted to let loose this hurricane, but at the same time also to stave it off. His plays constantly anticipate the "collapse of all those fictitious forms." This is done to such an extent in *Each in His Own Way* that even the expected angry reaction of audience and critics is momentarily reflected on the stage.

In the dramatic interludes the play presents a fictitious audience who debate about the play, are divided into pro- and anti-Pirandello factions, and at the same time see the story they have just watched on the stage take place among themselves in two of their number, Amelia Moreno and Baron Nuti.

By the model of this performing audience—they become machinelike in line with typical patterns of mass hysteria and can only throw out excited shouts and questions—Pirandello shows his intention, which is to throw his audience off balance. He wanted to move constantly from the level of theater to that of reality until, in the words of the Fourth Critic, it is as though they are "looking into a mirror that had somehow gone crazy. . . ." Thus, they are completely involved in Pirandello's anarchic experience, in an irrationality normally concealed from them behind the routine of convention.

It is true that the real challenge, the leaping over of the drama to the spectators, was not successful in *Each in His Own Way*. Unlike *Six Characters*, it led to no scandal when it was first produced in Milan in 1924. The audience enthusiastically applauded its derision and felt flattered by a dramatist who had by then become world famous and to whom it willingly allowed certain eccentricities and whims. "Pirandellism" had become fashionable, even conventional. And besides, all the critical arguments had already been advanced in the play itself. Thus, discussion was robbed of its sting and turned into a game.

It cannot be mere chance that the play has seldom been performed since then. In Italy it was not offered again until 1961, twenty-five years after Pirandello's death. In German it was performed for the first time in 1959 in Zurich. One of its rare English-language productions was offered, under the direction of Robert Winston, at an Edinburgh Festival.

This restraint is not only due to the fact that the play has a cast of more than fifty characters. More important is the fact that its over-calculated effect dissolves into nothingness. Its shock effect is no longer experienced as assaultive by the audience. Instead they recognize it, from the comfortable distance of their seats in the auditorium, and see through it as stage technique. The excessive proximity of stage and audience prevents all possibility of dramatic effectiveness.

Nevertheless, it is valid to say, as Luigi Squarzina,

the director of the production at the Teatro Stabile of Genoa, asserted, that this play revealed the "great Pirandello who resembles Joyce, Kafka, and Musil." "In this play," he said in justification of this view, "Pirandello integrated his poetic art with his dramatic work and anticipated the treatment of reality on various fragmentary levels, which is the characteristic of all great art in this century." That he thereby penetrated to the limits of dramatic possibility makes his plays, like the plays of Antonin Artaud and the ideas of Craig or Meyerhold, difficult to produce, but makes them historically significant for the future of the theater.

Tonight We Improvise

CONTENTS: The play begins in the auditorium. The start of the performance is delayed. Noise comes from the stage, and some of the actors, who are mingling with the audience, make loud protests. This gives the director, Dr. Hinkfuss, who suddenly storms onto the stage, the opportunity to make a dramatic entrance. He gets involved in a dispute with the angry spectators, in which he develops, in an aggressive and doctrinaire manner, his theory of the theater as a creation of the director. He looks on the work of the dramatist as so much raw material that he wants to make an effective stage reality. For this purpose he has divided a story of Pirandello's into a series of different images that the actors are to develop, without prior preparation, before the eyes of the spectators.

But this "miracle," which Hinkfuss wants to create by technical means and the spontaneity of the actors' performances, is not successful. In the course of the strained work of improvisation, the construction of the images and the entrances blur into each other in a curious maze. Only the director's explanations and the actors' remarks give any indication of what it is all about.

A family is shunned by Sicilian society on account of their life style. The mother and her four daughters lead a gay life with friends of the family, handsome air-force officers, while the father consoles himself in a nightclub and falls unhappily in love with a singer there. This love leads to his death. He is stabbed in defending the singer against an over-forward guest. His family, impoverished and shunned, sinks into misfortune. Mommina, the oldest daughter, tries to rescue them by marrying Verri, the most solid of the officers. But her marriage turns into a terrible prison, and she is being tortured to distraction by Verri's jealousy.

Only fragments of this Sicilian tragedy appear on the stage, and in the course of the play they disintegrate, giving way to a series of theatrical effects and to declamations by the actors that are totally centered on themselves. Finally, Hinkfuss is driven off by the actors, and the actress playing Mommina finishes the play with so pathetic an outburst, offered so movingly, that she herself almost dies of it, thus necessarily bringing the performance to an end.

What Pirandello unsuccessfully attempted in *Each in His Own Way* he was able to achieve five years later in *Tonight We Improvise*, the third of his play-within-the-play trilogy. *Tonight We Improvise* was premiered in January 1930 at the Neues Schauspielhaus in Königsberg. It gave rise to a considerable scandal when it was performed later that year at the

Lessingtheater in Berlin. This did not, like *Six Characters*, lead to an international success. What it did effect
at long last, as Herbert Ihering observed with satisfaction, was the long-awaited end to the Pirandello
fashion. The spiral of exaggerated theatricality, to
which Pirandello gave yet another twist in this play,
had by now gone too far: the public was tired of
Pirandello's shadowboxing.

At the very point in the final scene at which the
play once more genuinely appeals to the audience's
emotions, the spectators rose up in rebellion. And the
irony reached its high point when the hysteria this
time really moved from the auditorium to the stage,
when the actress broke out in real tears, and the
director in genuine rage called the audience irreverent
names.

This was not the scandal Pirandello wanted, least of
all in Germany, which had always received his plays
with such enthusiasm. *Tonight We Improvise* could
find no theater in Italy. It was no accident that it had
been completed in Berlin and provided with a dedication to Max Reinhardt, whose "unequaled creative
power had given magical life to *Six Characters in
Search of an Author* on the German stage."

Here in Berlin, Pirandello believed himself still
understood. His disappointment at his failure was all
the greater. He suffered, a friend reported, "all the
humiliations of a beginner." But what made him most
indignant was the intellectual crudity with which not
only the play itself but also the aesthetic theory put
forward in it was rejected.

Perhaps this very sensitivity betrays something of
the play's tendencies to abstraction. In *Six Characters*

and *Each in His Own Way* real feeling, ultimately emanating from Pirandello himself, was clearly evident behind all the theorizing and the technical expertise. But hardly any of this is apparent in *Tonight We Improvise*.

The theme of jealousy is here derived more from verismo than from Pirandello's own experience. It is crudely superficial and is not explored with insight. This time Pirandello was not interested in a drama of persons but in the drama of production. His play is only concerned with itself. No longer struggling against the intractability of the material, the play uses the intractability with a self-engrossed autonomy.

This too has an autobiographical basis. Parts of the play derive from Pirandello's own experiences as director in the years 1925 to 1928, when he directed the company of the Teatro d'Arte. But external influences are also more evident here than in his other plays.

The international success of *Six Characters* had introduced Pirandello to the most important theaters of Europe and America. He had come to know the extravaganzas and grandiloquent ideas of Pitoëff and Reinhardt, the theories of Yevreinov, and the revolutionary tendencies of the Russian stage generally, which proclaimed, under the influence of Tairov and Meyerhold, the return of the theater as theater. Meyerhold's statement in his essay on the theater of "deliberate convention"—the actor frees himself from his dependence on the director, as the latter frees himself from his dependence on the playwright—can be used as a motto for Pirandello's own play.

Many of Meyerhold's inventions—the use of stage

lighting to increase dramatic effectiveness, the elimi-
nation of the stage apron, the emphasis on décor, the
melodious declamation of dialogue—are demonstrated
in *Tonight We Improvise*. Even the inclusion of the
audience in the play, which Pirandello here employed
in an even more radical manner than in *Each in His
Own Way*, had been anticipated by Meyerhold, who
saw the spectator as "co-creator of the play," and
further developed by Yevreinov. For Yevreinov,
whom Pirandello enthusiastically greeted as a "friend
and soulmate," the whole world is a stage on which
men, animals, and plants play their part. The theater's
job is to transform the play into life, and life into the
play, by persuading the audience to take part in it
through total identification with the performance.

There is no doubt that all these ideas impelled and
encouraged Pirandello in his own experiments. Indeed,
they were probably responsible for the very existence
of this play, with which Pirandello, who was still being
accused of a certain provincialism despite his world-
wide reputation, wanted to demonstrate that he
belonged among the international avant-garde.

Despite this, it is unmistakably Pirandello himself
who here made use of these bold innovations. The
effects of "total theater" seem curiously changed in
him. They do not, as with the Russians, subordinate
themselves to an idea that brings everything—properties, décor, actors, text—into a strict unity. Instead
they acquire their own independence, turn into individual details, which, isolated from one another as
alien bodies, stand alongside and opposed to each
other.

Thus, at the beginning of the first scene a Sicilian

procession moves to the sound of bells and organ
music through the auditorium onto the stage, and as
it is disappearing there, the sound of jazz begins to be
heard. One side of the stage becomes transparent, and
through the gauze one can see the brightly lighted,
many-colored interior of a nightclub, in which a singer
in black veils, with white face and closed eyes, is
crooning a melancholy song. Somewhere about is one
of the characters in the play—Sampognetta, the father
of the family. A neighbor is at the point of putting a
pair of horns cut out of paper on him.

In the second scene the family can be seen in a
brightly lighted box at the opera. Simultaneously, a
silent film of a Verdi opera is shown on the stage,
accompanied by music on a record player. In the
intermission the actors continue to act their parts as
spectators among the other spectators in the lobby.
This coincides with a special performance by the
director, who puts on an "unusual play" by assembling
before the eyes of the spectators remaining in the
auditorium the set of an airport with low hangars,
small airplanes, and a starry sky. Then he takes it all
down again because he has no proper use for it.

And so it goes on—with stage effects always present
in the form of pure décor, when meaning ceases.

In another scene Ignazia, the mother in the family,
is praying under a delicate green spotlight that "represents something like an emanation of hope for the
intervention of a miracle." She recites a Hail Mary
for relief from toothache but is interrupted by the
sudden flash and noise of a red light as her daughter
enters, singing and in costume. On the other hand,
the death of Sampognetta in the same scene, dramatic

climax par excellence, with blood and tears, is totally lacking in tragic elements.

His entrance is delayed because the others, totally dependent on their enjoyment of the play, will not bring their own performance to an end, and the actor playing Sampognetta, annoyed, loses the desire to die. While the others wait nervously for the words of his dying monologue, he is silent and smiles, lets them wait, until eventually he describes at great length, in the subjunctive, the bravura with which he would have performed his death scene. Thus he dies.

A grotesque parody is all that remains in this play of the revolution of the theater. Pirandello was fascinated by the theories of production but mistrusted them. Despite its dedication to Reinhardt, who deeply impressed Pirandello, *Tonight We Improvise* is one long attack on Reinhardt as producer. The Austrian critic Alfred Polgar criticized Reinhardt's productions with these words—"It is a style that, haunted perhaps by the vision of 'shooting to kill,' feels the killing to be secondary; the flash and noise, the shape of the pistol, are the really important and fascinating elements." This approach is exaggerated to absurdity by Pirandello and made ridiculous.

The stunted body of Hinkfuss the director, a dwarf with enormous head and delicate fingers, as hairy as a caterpillar, is an indication of the value Pirandello placed upon a deliberately artificial and artistic arrangement of the stage. Nevertheless, he identified even with him. In the prologue, Hinkfuss sets out Pirandello's own theories of art and life: "But only under one condition, ladies and gentlemen, can something that art has given a seemingly unchangeable form be brought to life again, and once again set in motion to be made malleable. The condition is that it receives its impetus from us, a constantly new, changing, momentary life, a life that each of us is capable of giving it."

But this does not include the contradiction that is equally valid for Pirandello—that the transposition of art into life is not possible because life, the moment it appears on the stage, bursts out of its restrictive framework and takes on a chaotic state.

It is this idealistic theory of art that constantly reverses the director's intention, controls improvisation, and turns the effort into purely theatrical thunder. Nevertheless, despite his critical objections to the theater, Pirandello also made a discovery. He realized that the theater is the "wide-open jaws of a great machine: it suffers from a hunger that the playwrights do not know how to still."

The limitlessly increasing potential of theater was a challenge, and Pirandello met it with a brilliant stream of ideas, even though by way of parody. This playful mood, once liberated, drove him further forward than those who exerted the original stimulus. In his works theater becomes a self-enclosed system, a variegated spectacle. At points the elements of play completely stop and become self-suggestive and precursors of the happening. The moving procession, the explosion, the blinding flash, and, especially, the surprising and unrelated building and dismantling of the airport are solely intended, by means of a sudden dissociated physical effect, to assault the spectators. Unrelated elements are employed by Pirandello with full deliberation as new dramatic possibilities. Their function is to dupe the spectator by offering him an absurd experience that is not followed with further explanation.

The ultimate limit of dramatic possibility is reached with this extreme use of external effects. But the opposite attempt, to rescue the performance by means of a new internalization, also is confronted by these limitations of dramatic possibility. The actors respond to this "spectacle for the eye" with a revolt of the "heart"; they want to play what they "feel."

Without a director, without being tied to a prepared text, the actors present the death scene of Mommina —the drama of a broken heart. But at the point at which inner life takes over the production, and despair seeks for the most direct expression, the play falls apart. The final act takes place several years later. Mommina, alone with her children, in an almost bare stage setting (the walls of her inner prison, symbolically hinted at, are lighted up from time to time), falls plaintively into the role of the gipsy Azucena from Verdi's opera, *Il Trovatore*.

Singing and narrating, identifying herself more and more with the operatic role, she "performs" to her children until she reaches Azucena's song "Now the hour of death is near, everlasting rest beckons to me." While singing this aria, she dies. And it is precisely this cliché-ridden death scene that is no longer histrionic but real or almost real. The actress playing Mommina has a heart attack.

The play comes to an end here, at a point similar to that at which *Six Characters* ends. Where distance is abolished, and identification of art and life too intensely sought, theater is no longer possible. The result was not new for Pirandello. This time new means were used to achieve the result. Pirandello handled them with virtuosity but remained curiously aloof from the pyrotechnics of his own imagination. And even the carefully worked-out theories that he propounded yet again, as though he was writing his testament, give the impression, in contrast with the *Six Characters*, of being mechanically recited.

All this is part of the play's general tendency, but it is also a symptom of an increasing loss of substance and theme. In his later work Pirandello no longer attained the dramatic involvement of his earlier plays. Instead he gained something else—a greater independence from the conventional modes, a detachment that permitted him to be in sole custody of a theater that was becoming modern, more sophisticated, and more flexible.

In the fall of 1959, the Living Theater, an ensemble group committed to experimental and avant-garde theater, offered a new, well-regarded production of *Tonight We Improvise*. Julian Beck and Judith Malina, the intrepid co-producers of the Living Theater, were cast as the director and as Mommina, respectively. Brooks Atkinson dredged up kinder words for the production than for the play, ending his review (*New York Times*, 7 November 1959) with these words: "Although the play is valueless and largely incomprehensible, the inquiry is interesting."

Earlier in the review Mr. Atkinson wrote:

> [Tonight We Improvise] begins with sounds of quarreling backstage before the curtains are parted. In the role of Director, Mr. Beck appears

before the curtains, reproves the actors and tells the audience what to expect. Impertinent people in the audience answer him rudely. Finally, the actors come before the audience like a group of sullen, bickering, unruly egotists, object to the nature of their profession, which destroys their own personality, and then begin to act a play about a volatile Sicilian family.

The main body of the play is negligible. Pirandello uses it as something to be tossed around in search of the nature of truth. In the second act when the improvisations and little side games are abandoned, the main body of the play gets dull. . . .

But in the first act, when Mr. Beck is holding the audience at bay, and the actors are wrangling in the aisles and giving him a hard time, "Tonight We Improvise" is amusing.

While other critics handled it as a serious theater event, disentangling farce and meaning, examining what Pirandello was saying about the dramatist, the actor, and the theater, Whitney Bolton (New York *Morning Telegraph*, 9 November 1959) threw up his hands, writing:

I haven't the slightest idea what they were doing or why they were doing it, but we all had a great time of it from first to last. . . . Julian Beck and his people, all mad as hatters and twice as noisy . . . do everything but sit in the laps of the audience and Opening Night a couple of them tried that. This is riot and tumult, fun and frolic, impudence and audacity.

The Mountain Giants

CONTENTS: A theatrical company that has known better days appears one evening in the imaginary kingdom of the Ravens of Misfortune, a curious society of the dispersed, who live, in an ownerless villa, a life given over to dreams and illusions.

Cotrone, magician and head of the Ravens of Misfortune, introduces the actors to the wonders of this phantom world, conjures up voices, magic lights, and the missing actors of the play *The Fable of the Changeling Son*, with which the company, in the meantime shrunk in numbers, has been touring unsuccessfully for months. Only here, in the villa, explains Cotrone, can the fable come to life. But Ilse, the guiding spirit of the theatrical company, insists on bringing the play to the people. The dramatist, who had loved her and written the play for her, but whom she had rejected, had hanged himself in despair at his unrequited love. Since then she feels it her sacred duty to turn the fable into a success.

Her husband, the count, who runs the company with her, has spent his fortune on producing the play. Now they want to make a final attempt to put on the play at the marriage of the Giants who are engaged in an enormous project on the mountain—the diverting of the water into sandy basins, the building of factories and streets, and the construction of an agricultural society. Cotrone takes them to the Giants, who permit the play to be shown to their people but do not themselves attend.

The people, dulled and coarsened by total preoccupation with material things, make fun of the play. But Ilse does not give in: she wants art to be victorious. She is unsuccessful, allows herself to be so carried away by anger that she abuses the people, and is killed by the mob.

The Mountain Giants, Pirandello's last play, enjoys the almost legendary reputation of a great unfinished work that had occupied Pirandello's imagination to the end of his life. It was after his death therefore given to the world as it were like a bequest.

On the evening before he died, Pirandello dictated to his son a resumé of the third act, which he intended to write out in full within the following few days. What we have today are two unrevised acts, and the plan of the final part, which was to have led to the dramatic climax, the collision of the theater with the world of Giants. This is little enough for a performance. Nevertheless, after an unsuccessful open-air production in Florence in 1937, the play was successfully staged by Giorgio Strehler. He managed to transform the available material into an impressive visionary spectacle. This production has contributed to the guarded respect with which critics have regarded Strehler since then.

This final play of Pirandello's belongs among those plays that he himself called "miti" (myths). Earlier he had completed *The New Colony* and *Lazarus*. Pirandello evidently planned, under the influence of fascism and after the breakup of his own theatrical company in 1928, to develop a theater that came closer to the people's own imagination and reacquainted them with their own native spirit.

At any rate that is how one can understand the statement he made in 1929 about the "primitive and natural forms of the spirit." These forms, he said, in an interview with *Il Corriere della Sera*, were a victory of the spirit for as long as they remained living expressions. To tear them down for the pleasure of replacing them with new forms was destructive of the human spirit and thus a crime. Certain primitive yet natural forms of expression employed by the human spirit were not to be set aside since in them life expressed itself in a natural way. He used these myths, as he wrote elsewhere, whose origins were the "elemental and irreversible changes of the earthly cycle—ascendance and descent, birth and death"—to address himself by their means to "all mortal creatures."

This is a highly remarkable, most un-Pirandellian statement, a complete reversal of what he had done in the theater until then—which was the creation of a passionately intellectual drama resulting from the experience of tension between "life" and "form."

His romantic striving to get close to the sources of the people's imagination must soon have given him

cause to think. At least he must have reflected after he
had noticed that his "myths" found absolutely no echo
in the people. In 1933 he again made the attempt with
The Fable of the Changeling Son, an opera libretto
(with music by Gian Francesco Malipiero) the subject
of which he took from the motif of an Italian fairy
tale. The opera was not only prohibited by the Nazis
after its original German production in Braunschweig
in 1934, at which Hitler was present, but also failed
immediately afterward in Rome, in Mussolini's pres-
ence.

The German prohibition was due to a misunder-
standing. They resented the fact that the weak-
minded was characterized as a Northerner, and the
changeling son, who was to inherit the throne in his
place, as a handsome, Mediterranean youth. Pirandello protested that all this was only a *fable,* without
implications of any kind. But in Rome, too, they
wanted to know nothing about this fable. And Pirandello was left with the impression that the artist's
mythologizing imagination would have no chance in
the new technocratic world of the dictatorships.

One has to be familiar with this early history to
understand the intentions of *The Mountain Giants.*
What Pirandello shows us in this play is the dilemma
of the writer who has lost his platform. He criticizes
the crudity of a mass culture that, in the effort
required for material construction, has strongly developed its physical powers but has spiritually become a
little dull and coarse.

The village the company visits has a theater, it is
true, "but only for the mice." "Even if it were open,
no one would go inside." They want to tear it down

in order to build a small stadium for races and wrestling or to build up a cinema. These are allusions to the pleasure cult, hostile to the arts, that fascism had set up for the masses.

The criticism, however, that Pirandello leveled at the play and at himself is of a more subtle kind. *The Mountain Giants* is called a "myth" in the subtitle, but what it demonstrates is the failure of myth in art. The Ravens of Misfortune, who populate Cotrone's villa, are people who have come down in the world: Sigricia, to whom the One Hundred and One Angel had prophesied death and who continues to exist only as someone who has died; Quaqueo, the fat dwarf in a child's dress; Mara-Mara, the "blown-up rubber lady"; Maria Maddalena, a poor madwoman who roams over the fields, making herself available to the men and abandoning her children. These are in part figures from Sicilian myths, in part pure "inventions," as Cotrone says, and in part, as for example "My Little Lord," Duccio Doccia, and Cotrone, grotesque mythical images of Pirandello himself.

Their contact with the world is broken; they live only in themselves, "stripped of everything," but surrounded by an "immeasurable richness of bubbling dreams." In their aloofness from human society they have themselves returned to nature, "pure as the ether, filled with sun and clouds." They sit there and imagine themselves in competition with the spirits of nature to whom they give meaning through their magic. But the marvels of this world of myths and magic, which Cotrone conjures up with his chanting, are simply products of a nihilistic despair. The Ravens of Misfortune no longer seek for reasons, they no longer explain anything. Instead, with quiet desperation they give the things that surround them a quite arbitrary meaning, for "one cannot live on nothing," says Cotrone.

It is the mind freed from all social and metaphysical ties that here toys with itself. Its creations are phantoms, fragmented dreams, ghosts that transform truth and all external reality into ephemeral fantasies and transient shadows.

The shimmering kingdom of the Ravens of Misfortune, filled with a heavenly intoxication, is a world of the dead, peopled by shadows, which in their turn invent other shadows in the endless process of a disillusion that cannot escape from illusion. Being without external restraints, it falls victim to imagination run wild.

The advantage for the stage is that Pirandello, like Strindberg, developed a special dramatic technique to portray this state of mind cut off from all contact— the dramatic technique of the dream. He let dreams and imagination act independently, giving them a reality that transforms the stage into a phantasmagoria.

The second act, a night scene, takes us into the center of the villa—the "arsenal of appearances." Here the objects of the imagination are simply lying around in the form of rubbish—dolls and ninepins with human faces, curious domestic appliances, unreal furniture that is dusty and discarded playthings. Everything is illuminated with an indefinable light.

On the back wall of the room, which is transparent, the pictures change as in a dream. A sky is seen in the reddish glow of dawn, the gentle slope of a mountain in delicate green, a bay with harbor and lighthouse.

The people who enter here become figures in a dream revealing their own fears and desires: the count confesses his unsuccessful wooing of his wife; Spizzi, one of the actors, who is also unhappily in love with the countess, hangs himself, thus repeating once more, at the level of the imagination, the death of the artist. Other actors mingle in costume with the dolls, who suddenly come to life and dance with jerky movements, while the ninepins leap around with heads held high, the trumpet blares forth, and the drum sets up a rat-tat-tat without drumstick.

Everything moves in a disorderly fashion, according to some confused unharmonious pattern. Sigricia appears with the One Hundred and One Angel; a wall opens and a dwarf can be seen handing Maria Maddalena a little box; music comes out of a fountain and suddenly ceases.

This play, made up of witchery and tricks, not only appears to anticipate the theater of the absurd, but also destroys it. The dramatic technique of the dream, introduced by Strindberg and held together by him, despite a seeming lack of cohesion, by the logic of inner life, dissolves with Pirandello into a medley of wild juggleries. It is theater at the lowest level, diffuse and distorted puppet theater. Pirandello's clear rejection of this dream theater, as exemplifying the work of the writer isolated by society, is plain.

The stage has turned into a lumber room, into ironic laughter at the meaninglessness of the world of the imagination. Of this world Cotrone says, "Perhaps the most necessary element is lacking in us, but everything superfluous is richly present." By this Pirandello was also referring to his own unhappy attempts to let his art revert to "natural" poetry.

The puppets, properties, and décor are the materials of his *Fable of the Changeling Son*. Everything is so arranged that at the wave of a hand, on a single command, the materials can become the setting for the *Fable*. And when Ilse, urged by Cotrone, begins to recite her part, surrounded by the dream scenery, there suddenly stand before her in a magical light the figures of the Two Women Neighbors from the play. They play their part with her. Here art turns into pure reflection of itself, to an isolated will-o'-the-wispish reflex. It is "like a miracle," says Cotrone, "that is sufficient in itself, without demanding from any one that he should understand it."

Pirandello's relationship to this isolated world of art was ambivalent. He was fascinated, but at the same time kept at a distance. To cut himself off, to flee embittered into the protective vacuum of his fantastic inspirations, was for him doubtless a great attraction after the recent years of disappointment. Indicative of this is what he wrote at the time: "Nowadays I prefer dreams to reality. Almost all that I see repels me. More than ever am I afraid of life. Nevertheless, I am also strangely joyful at the certainty I now have that whatever human there is in us is of least importance."

He was filled, as Franz Rauhut says in his book *The Young Pirandello*, with a pantheistic intoxication "to become one with the sun." This is the one striking parallel with the early Camus, whose asocial and absurd sense of life found an effusive rapturous expression in a sun cult.

The return both to nature and to the unfettered inventive imagination were Pirandello's reactions to a deep hurt, a deep-rooted doubt in the possibility of a successful human relationship. But right to the very end something different from the temptation to seek refuge in resignation was working in him: his desire to communicate himself, "to go to the end of the world in the service of his work. As a human being who is able to say something important to other human beings, not as preacher, for heaven's sake, but as artist—to create beauty that is precisely the beauty of truth made alive."

In *The Mountain Giants*, this messianic urge to communicate contradicts a misanthropic dream world. But it too becomes grotesquely distorted in the world of the theater, split between art and society, between spirit and matter.

Ilse, the embodiment of missionary sense, is a disturbed and hysterical tragedian who lets herself be carried through the countryside, feverish and lying on a hay wagon, in a worn purple dress. Obsessed by her monomania, she recites her part in the *Fable* when they arrive at the villa. Torn from its context, it seems meaningless, its sole virtue a certain declamatory power. This role and the fanaticism that will not allow her to relinquish her quest for an audience for the play are her whole life. For the rest, everything since the dramatist's death is "like a dream or another life. A life after death. . . ."

Art has taken the place of life with an all-exclusiveness that gives it a sacred character, turns it into a holy trust to which Ilse finally sacrifices herself when she appears before the people of the Giants. But her monomania makes any real contact with the people all the more impossible. The histrionic seriousness, which Ilse brings to the play, only increases the distance between the people and the play and makes the chasm between them still deeper. The opposition of the two worlds becomes clear, noted Pirandello: "On the one side are the fanatics of art, who consider themselves sole keepers of the spirit; and on the other, there is the incomprehension of the masses who despise them."

This conflict is deadly to art. Ilse dies at the hands of the incensed crowd. "The poor fanatical servants of life," Pirandello explained at the end, "in whom the spirit is silent, but some day capable of speaking, have in blind fury crushed the fanatical servants of art, who are not understood by the masses because they turn their backs on real life and because they do not keep their dreams to themselves but always try to thrust them onto others."

This self-critical assertion, so destructive to art but on the other hand so promising for the audience, remained Pirandello's last word on the theater. There is something he seems to have suppressed in the hastily dictated final act—the aggressive impulse of the play, whose original intention is evident in the invention of the Giants with their dull, unthinking brutality.

The Giants do not appear at all in the final sketch of the third act. At most they provide the opportunity, by their nonappearance, for what happens. But one of the earlier versions had envisaged a different function for the Giants. In this version there was to have appeared from time to time over the curtain behind which the actors put on their costumes a "grinning Giant's head." And for the fourth act, the directions are: "As soon as the performance begins, the Giant's interruptions begin too." Clearly, Pirandello had first thought to turn the Giants themselves into grotesque opponents of art. It seems safe to assume his own negative experience under Hitler and Mussolini had in this play burst forth.

Pirandello had come to view with deep suspicion the favor shown to the arts by the fascist state. Something of this can also be seen in his final summary. After the actress's death the steward was to appear and hand over a large sum of money as compensation. With this money was to be built a tomb to the death of poetry. In this allegory the hidden intention of the play is once more evident—criticism of a state in whose philistine climate of terror nothing remained of art save ostentatious decoration.

More than other Pirandello plays, this one requires supplemental imaginative powers from the director. The text is only partly there; the story line lacks scenic weight, has no high points or rhythm. There are surrealistlike confusion in the second act and a pantomimelike finish that shows Ilse's murder in shadow play. The whole is an imaginative hocus-pocus, with deeper meaning hidden in the performance and dialogue. To create this twilight dimension without falling into deep-seated gloom or mere manipulation is difficult. Giorgio Strehler, director of Milan's Pic-

colo Teatro, in his so far almost unrivaled production
of the play, not only avoided both pitfalls but also
turned the play into what is only hinted at in the text
—a magical, visionary, poetic dream play.

Opinions on this experiment are various. Alfred Polgar, who saw Strehler's production in the Zurich
Schauspielhaus, was skeptical:

> It is extremely doubtful whether the spectator
> whose first encounter with *The Mountain Giants*
> is in the theater will be able genuinely to relate
> to it either by understanding or empathy. It is
> very seldom that a sudden illuminating flash of
> dialogue lights up the intellectual landscape of
> the play, which is engaged in a dance of the
> seven veils in reverse, always wrapping one more
> around itself. . . . The production, colorful and
> individualistic as it is, unfortunately does not ease
> the path to understanding the secrets of *The
> Mountain Giants* (though it is doubtful whether
> any production would be able to do this). In that
> of the Schauspielhaus, there was much shouting
> and whispering. Long monologues were whis-
> pered rather than spoken aloud. And this made
> understanding difficult in a double sense—under-
> standing the words said and understanding the
> meaning.

The enthusiasm of the critics after Strehler's production in the Schauspielhaus at Düsseldorf in 1958 was
unanimous. This time Bernhard Minetti played
Cotrone and Maria Wimmer the countess. The critics
spoke of a "marvel of spiritual artistry" (Albert

Schulze Vellinghausen), of the "discovery of fascinating powers of the imagination" (Siegfried Melchinger).

> What Strehler manages to extract, as if by magic from the German company, in precise movements and sudden standstill, in flexibility of voice and words, in intensity of emotion, can only receive our grateful admiration. . . . In Minetti's acting Pirandello's richly intellectual facility only rises to truly sublime heights by slow degrees, after first being worked out cerebrally. . . .

In April 1961 the Living Theater offered two dramatic readings of this play, an experiment that critic Arthur Gelb called "a satisfactory one," going on to say that the performance was certainly "a must for all sincere avant-gardists."

In his review in the *New York Times*, Mr. Gelb wrote:

> It would be hard to imagine a more appropriate showcase of style [than that of the Living Theater] for this strange work. . . . In keeping with the Living Theater's tradition of audience participation, the action is briefly carried into the auditorium, blessedly interrupting a particularly talky stretch in the third act. And the problem of the unwritten fourth act is solved by the narrator, George Miller, who delivers a running commentary based on Stefano's notes. This is interspersed with bits of dialog and formalized movement by members of Lionel Shepard's mime group.

About this presentation Bernard Krisher (*New York World-Telegram*) wrote:

> Many ideas are thrown about between the actors and their hosts, including opinions on the nature of poetry, the truth of dreams, the insensitivity of the masses toward art and the inability of actors to bridge the gap which exists between art and the people. All this could be quite dull for two hours, if Pirandello's wit did not intrude from time to time and if the acting were not so superb.

Both critics praised the performance of Judith Malina as the countess, Ilse.

BIBLIOGRAPHY

1. PLAYS BY PIRANDELLO

All for the Best—*Tutto per bene*. Translation by Henry Reed, in *Right You Are! (If You Think So)*, Penguin Books, 1962.

As Well as Before, Better than Before—*Come prima, meglio di prima*.

As You Desire Me—*Come tu mi vuoi*. Translation by Marta Abba, in *Twenty Best European Plays on the American Stage*, edited by J. Gassner, New York: Crown Publishers, 1957.

At the Gate—*All'uscita*. Translation in *The One-Act Plays of Luigi Pirandello*, New York: Dutton, 1928.

Bellavita—*Bellavita*. Translation by William Murray, in *Pirandello's One-Act Plays*, Garden City, New York: Doubleday (Anchor Books), 1964.

Birds That Fly High—*Gli uccelli dell'alto*.

But It Is Not a Serious Affair—*Ma non è una cosa seria*.

Cap and Bells—*Il berretto a sonagli*.

Chee-Chee—*Cecè*. Translation by William Murray, in *Pirandello's One-Act Plays*, Garden City, New York: Doubleday (Anchor Books), 1964.

Diana and Tuda—*Diana e la Tuda*. Translation by Marta Abba, New York: Samuel French, 1960.

The Doctor's Duty—*Il dovere del medico*. Translation in *The One-Act Plays of Luigi Pirandello*, New York: Dutton, 1928.

Each in His Own Way—*Ciascuno a suo modo*. Translation by Arthur Livingston, in *Naked Masks*, edited by Eric Bentley, New York: Dutton (Everyman's Library), 1952.

Either of One or of No One—*O di uno o di nessuno*.

The Fable of the Changeling Son—*La favola del figlio cambiato*.

The Festival of Our Lord of the Ship—*Sagra del Signore della nave*. Translation in *The Nobel Prize Treasury*, edited by M. McClintock, Garden City, New York: Doubleday, 1948.

Grafting—*L'innesto*.

Henry IV—*Enrico IV*. Translation by Edward Storer, in *Makers of the Modern Theater*, edited by B. Ulanov, New York: McGraw-Hill, 1961. Also, translation, "The Emperor," by Eric Bentley, in *The Genius of the Italian Theatre*, New York: New American Library, 1964.

If Not So, or Other People's Reasons—*Se non così, o La ragione degli altri*.

The Imbecile—*L'imbecille*. Translation in *The One-Act Plays of Luigi Pirandello*, New York: Dutton, 1928.

I'm Dreaming, But Am I?—*Sogno (ma forse no)*. Translation by William Murray, in *Pirandello's One-Act Plays*, Garden City, New York: Doubleday (Anchor Books), 1964.

The Jar—*La giara*. Translation by William Murray, in *Pirandello's One-Act Plays*, Garden City, New York: Doubleday (Anchor Books), 1964.

Lazarus—*Lazzaro*. Translation in *Three Plays*, Penguin Books, 1959.

The License—*La patente*. Translation, "By the Judgment of the Court," in *The One-Act Plays of Luigi Pirandello*, New York: Dutton, 1928.

The Life I Gave You—*La vita che ti diedi*. Translation in *Three Plays*, Penguin Books, 1959.

Liolà—*Liolà*. Translation by Eric Bentley and Gerardo Guerrieri, in *Naked Masks*, edited by Eric Bentley, New York: Dutton (Everyman's Library), 1952.

Man, Beast, and Virtue—*L'uomo, la bestia, e la virtù*.

The Man with the Flower in His Mouth—*L'uomo dal fiore in bocca*. Translation in *The One-Act Plays of Luigi Pirandello*, New York: Dutton, 1928. Also, translation by Eric Bentley, in *Tulane Drama Review* 1, no. 3 (1957):15–22.

The Mountain Giants—*I giganti della montagna*. Translation by Marta Abba, in *The Mountain Giants, and Other Plays*, New York: Crown Publishers, 1958.

Mrs. Morli, One and Two—*La signora Morli, una e due*.

The New Colony—*La nuova colonia*. Translation by Marta Abba, in *The Mountain Giants, and Other Plays*, New York: Crown Publishers, 1958.

No One Knows How—*Non si sa come*. Translation by Marta Abba, New York: Samuel French, 1963.

The Other Son—*L'altro figlio*.

The Pleasure of Honesty—*Il piacere dell'onestà*. Translation by William Murray, in *To Clothe the Naked, and Two Other Plays*, New York: Dutton, 1962.

The Rehearsal: Dramatic Scenes—*Provando la commedia: Scene tetrali*.

Role Playing—*Il giuoco delle parti.* Translation, "The Rules of the Game," by William Murray, in *To Clothe the Naked, and Two Other Plays,* New York: Dutton, 1962.

Scamander—*Scamandro.*

Sicilian Limes—*Lumìe di Sicilia.* Translation by Isaac Goldberg, in *Plays of the Italian Theatre,* Boston: Luce, 1921. Also, translation by Robert Rietty, in *Limes from Sicily, and Other Plays,* Leeds: E. J. Arnold, 1967.

Six Characters in Search of an Author—*Sei personaggi in cerca d'autore.* Translation by Edward Storer, in *A Treasury of the Theater,* vol. 2, edited by J. Gassner, New York: Simon & Schuster, 1951. Adaptation by Paul Avila Mayer, in *Masterpieces of the Modern Italian Theatre,* edited by R. W. Corrigan, New York: Collier Books, 1967.

Think, Giacomino!—*Pensaci, Giacomino!*

Thus It Is (If It Seems So to You)—*Così è (se vi pare).* Translation, "Right You Are! (If You Think So)," by Arthur Livingston, in *Three Plays,* New York: Dutton, 1922. Also, translation, *Right You Are: A Stage Version,* by Eric Bentley, New York: Columbia University Press, 1954.

To Clothe the Naked—*Vestire gli ignudi.* Translation by William Murray, in *To Clothe the Naked, and Two Other Plays,* New York: Dutton, 1962.

To Find Oneself—*Trovarsi.* Translation by Marta Abba, New York: Samuel French, 1960.

Tonight We Improvise—*Questa sera si recita a soggetto.* Translation by Samuel Putnam, New York: Dutton, 1932. Also, translation by Marta Abba, New York: Samuel French, 1961.

The Vise—*La morsa.* Translation in *The One-Act*

Plays of Luigi Pirandello, New York: Dutton, 1928.

When Someone Is Somebody—*Quando si è qualcuno*. Translation by Marta Abba, in *The Mountain Giants, and Other Plays*, New York: Crown Publishers, 1958.

The Wives' Friend—*L'amica delle mogli*. Translation by Marta Abba, New York: Samuel French, 1960.

2. PIRANDELLO'S NONDRAMATIC WORKS IN TRANSLATION

NOVELS

The Outcast. Translated by Leo Ongley. New York: Dutton, 1925.

Shoot: The Notebooks of Serafino Gubbio, Cinematograph Operator. Translated by C. K. Scott Moncrieff. New York: Dutton, 1926.

One, None, and a Hundred Thousand. Translated by Samuel Putnam. New York: Dutton, 1933.

The Old and the Young. Translated by C. K. Scott Moncrieff. New York: Dutton, 1933.

The Late Mattia Pascal. Translated by William Weaver. New York: Doubleday, 1964.

SHORT-STORY COLLECTIONS

The Horse in the Moon: Twelve Short Stories. Translated by Samuel Putnam. New York: Dutton, 1932.

Better Think Twice about It, and Twelve Other Stories. Translated by Arthur and Henrie Mayne. New York: Dutton, 1934.

The Medals, and Other Stories. New York: Dutton, 1939.

Short Stories. Translated by Lily Duplaix. New York: Simon & Schuster, 1959.

The Merry-Go-Round of Love, and Selected Stories. Translated by Frances Keene and Lily Duplaix. New York: New American Library, 1964.

Short Stories. Translated by Frederick May. New York: Oxford University Press, 1964.

3. WORKS ABOUT PIRANDELLO

Bentley, Eric R. "Pirandello: Joy and Torment." In *In Search of Theater.* New York, 1953.

──────. *The Playwright as Thinker: A Study of Drama in Modern Times.* 8th edition. Cleveland and New York, 1963.

──────. "Il tragico imperatore." *Tulane Drama Review* 10, no. 3 (Spring 1966): 60–75.

Bishop, Thomas. *Pirandello and the French Theater.* New York, 1960.

Büdel, Oscar. *Pirandello: Studies in Modern European Thought and Literature.* New York, 1966.

Cambon, Glauco, ed. *Pirandello: A Collection of Critical Essays.* Englewood Cliffs, N.J., 1967.

Croce, Benedetto. "Pirandello." In *La letteratura della nuova Italia,* vol. 6. Bari, 1946.

Ferrante, L. *Luigi Pirandello.* Florence, 1958.

Illiano, Antonio. "Pirandello in England and the United States: A Chronological List of Criticism." *Bulletin of the New York Public Library,* February 1967.

Lo Vecchio Musti, M. *Bibliografia di Pirandello.* 2nd edition. Milan, 1952.

Lucas, F. L. *Drama of Chekhov, Synge, Yeats, and Pirandello.* London, 1963.

MacClintock, Lander. *The Age of Pirandello.* Bloomington, Ind., 1951.

Poggioli, Renato. "Pirandello in Retrospect." In *The Spirit of the Letter*. Cambridge, Mass., 1965.

Rauhut, Franz. *Der junge Pirandello*. Munich, 1964. Also includes bibliography.

Starkie, Walter. *Luigi Pirandello: 1867–1936*. 3rd edition. Berkeley, 1965.

Vittorini, Domenico. *The Drama of Luigi Pirandello*. 2nd edition. New York, 1957.

William, Herman. "Pirandello and Possibility." *Tulane Drama Review* 10, no. 3 (Spring 1966).

INDEX

Abba, Marta, 29, 96, 98
Accademia d'Italia, 4, 17
adaptation to society
    necessity for, 5–6, 18
    problem of, in the plays,
        35–36, 41, 48–50, 71–
        73, 88, 106, 125, 137,
        138–39
Agata Renni, 68–75
Agazzi, Signor and Signora,
        43–53
Agrigento, Sicily, 1, 6
Amelia Moreno, 129–42
anarchical life force
    within the characters, 39–
        40, 41, 123, 134
    concept of, 12, 140
Andersen, Margarete, 54
Angelo Baldovino, 68–75
Antonelli, Luigi, 21
APA Repertory Company
        (New York), 58
apologist for reason, the,
        50–52, 136–40
Artaud, Antonin, 78, 142
As Well as Before, Better
        than Before, 3

Atkinson, Brooks, 56, 128,
        152–53

Bachmann, Claus-Henning,
        53
Ball, William, 101
Barnes, Clive, 67, 114–15,
        116
Barnowsky, Viktor, 112
Beatrice Fiorica, 33–42
Beaufort, John, 100–101
Beck, Julian, 152–53
Behrendt, Klaus, 54
Belcredi, Baron, 102–117
Benn, Gottfried, 138
Bentley, Eric, 29, 104
    production by, 57–58
    translations by, 58, 67, 114
Bergson, Henri, 10–11
Bijou Theater (New York),
        66
Birds That Fly High, 1, 20
Bolton, Whitney, 153
Brecht, Bertolt, 65
Brües, Otto, 99

Camus, Albert, 138, 161–62

Cap and Bells, 2, 3, 19, 33–42, 49
  synopsis of, 33–34
Capanetta, 1
Capuana, Luigi, 2
Carraro, Tino, illustration of, 61
Cavacchioli, Enrico, 21
Cherry Lane Theater (New York), 98
Chiarelli, Luigi, 21–22
Christian Science Monitor
  review from, excerpted, 100–101
Ciampa, 33–42, 49, 71
Colt, Alvin, 101
commedia dell'arte, 22, 25, 30, 53, 58, 93
communication
  impossibility of, 8–9, 75, 162
  inability of art in, 156–64 passim
Corriere della Sera, Il (newspaper)
  interview in, 156
Corsaro, Frank, 128
Cortese, Valentina, illustration of, 62
Cotrone, 154–67
Craig, Edward Gordon, 142
critical evaluation of productions, 27–28, 44–45, 53–58, 67, 95–101, 111–17, 128, 152–53, 165–67
Croce, Benedetto, 44–45

D'Annunzio, Gabriele, 17
Delia Morello, 129–42
dialect theater
  and Pirandello, 19, 33, 44
  in Sicily, 18–21

Diebold, Bernhard, 54
Diego Cinci, 129–42
  and Pirandello, 139
director, the (*Six Characters*), 76–101
Doro Palegari, 129–42
dramatic technique, 24–25, 37
  in *Cap and Bells*, 41
  in *Each in His Own Way*, 131
  of Meyerhold, 146–47
  in *Mountain Giants*, 159, 160
  in *Pleasure of Honesty*, 70, 72
  in *Six Characters*, 83, 86
  in *Thus It Is*, 50, 52–53
dramaturgy of Pirandello, 22–26, 146
  and *Cap and Bells*, 42
  and *Each in His Own Way*, 131–32, 138–39
  and Meyerhold, 146–47
  and *Pleasure of Honesty*, 69–70, 73, 74–75
  and *Six Characters*, 79, 81–83, 91–94
  and *Thus It Is*, 45, 51–53, 55
  and *To Clothe the Naked*, 120
  and Yevreinov, 147
Düggelin, Werner, 61
Dumas *fils*, Alexandre, 22

Each in His Own Way, 3, 129–42, 144, 146, 147
  innovations in, 135
  interview on, 139
  introduction to, 129
  productions of, 3, 141–42
  synopsis of, 129–31

Easley, Holmes, 58, 67
Eliot, T. S., 26
Epilogue, 20–21
Erfurth, Ulrich, 99–100
Ersilia Drei, 118–28
esclusa, L', 2
étranger, L' (Camus), 138

Fabio, 68–75
*Fable of the Changeling
    Son, The*, 4, 157, 161
  in *Mountain Giants*, 154
Fasci, the, 13–14, 15
fascism, 12–18
  and the arts, 158, 164
  and *Henry IV*, 110
  and *Mountain Giants*,
    158, 164
  and Pirandello, 3, 15–18,
    110, 156
Father, the, 76–101
Feist, Gene, 67
*Festival of Our Lord of the
    Ship, The*, 3
Finney, Albert, 115
Fleres, Ugo, 2
Ford, John, 78
Francesco Savio, 129–42
Franco Laspiga, 118–28
Franzen, Erich, 113
Frigerio, Jone, 97
Frola, Signora, 43–58, 67
fu Mattia Pascal, Il, 2, 19

Gabriel, Gilbert W., 56–57
Garibaldi, Giuseppe, 13
Gelb, Arthur, 166
Gelhart, Bebe, illustration
    of, 66
Giants, the, 154–64
Giovangigli, Orazio Costa,
    61

Giudice, Gaspare, 6–7
Göttinger Presse (news-
    paper)
  review from, excerpted,
    53–54
Grotti, Consul, 118–28
Gründgens, Gustaf, 113
Gülstorff, Max, 96, 97
Guthrie, Tyrone, 100–101

Haigh, Kenneth, 114–15
Harrison, Rex, 115–16
Hauptmann, Gerhart, 22
Hayes, Helen, 58
Hegel, Friedrich, 23
Henry IV, 102–117
Henry IV, 3, 69, 102–117,
    119, 123
  productions of, 3, 60–61,
    111–17
  and *Six Characters*, 105
  synopsis of, 102–103
Her Husband, 2
Herlie, Eileen, 116
Hinkfuss, Dr., 143–53
  and Pirandello, 149–50
Hitler, Adolf, 4, 157, 164
Höflich, Lucie, 97
Hollaender, Felix, 113
Holm, Klaus, 101
humor, essay on, 5, 11, 17,
    22–23

Ibsen, Henrik, 22, 53
identity. *See also* mask
  problem of, in the plays,
    71, 120–28 passim,
    133–34
*If Not So, or Other
    People's Reasons*, 2
Ignazia, 143–53
Ihering, Herbert, 145

illusion and reality, as
    theme, 102–111
    passim. *See also*
    reality
Ilse, 154–67
Ionesco, Eugène, 91
Italy, political life in, 12–18

Jacobs, Monty, 27
Joyce, James, 142
jugendstil, 11

Kafka, Franz, 142
Karsch, Walther, 99
Kates, Bernard, 128
Kerr, Walter, 116–17
Kinz, Franziska, 98
Klaar, Alfred, 96, 97, 112
Knopf, Julius, 111
Köppen, Franz, 95–96
Krisher, Bernard, 167

La Gioia, John, 67
Late Mattia Pascal, The, 2,
    19
Laudisi, 43–58
    and Diego Cinci, 136
Lazarus, 156
Leininger, Claus, 53–54
Liepman, Heinz, 113
Liolà, 2, 19
Little Boy, 76–101
Little Girl, 76–101
Little Huts, 1
Living Theater (New
    York), 152–53, 166–
    67
Ludovico Nota, 118–28
    and Pirandello, 121
Luft, Friedrich, 99

Mal giocondo, 1

Malina, Judith, 152–53, 167
Malipiero, Gian Francesco,
    157
Man, Beast, and Virtue, 3
Marshall, Armina, 56
Martoglio, Nino, 18–19
maschere nude, 5
mask, the
    characters' acceptance of,
        125–27, 133–34
    characters' construction
        of, 37–39, 48–50, 70–
        71, 102–111 passim
    concept of, 5, 114, 117
    of Pirandello, 18
    and the unmasking, 41,
        135
Mask and the Face, The
    (Chiarelli), 21
Mason, Reginald, 55–56
mass culture
    and the writer, 157–58
    and art, 163
Matilda, the Marchesa, 102–
    117
Matteotti, Giacomo, 16
Melchinger, Siegfried, 166
Mercer, Beryl, 56
    illustration of, 59
Meyer-Graefe, Julius, 28, 95
Meyerhold, Vsevolod, 142
    dramaturgy of, 146–47
Michele Rocca, 129–42
Miller, Betty, 58
Miller, George, 166
Minetti, Bernhard, 165, 166
    illustration of, 63
"miti," 156, 157
Moeller, Philip, 55–56, 59
Moissi, Alexander, 112–13
Mommina, 143–53
Mother, the, 76–101

Mountain Giants, The, 4, 16, 154–67
  fragments of, 154, 164
  productions of, 4, 62–63, 155–56, 164–67
  synopsis of, 154–55
Mrs. Morli, One and Two, 3
Münch, Richard, 99–100
Musco, Angelo, 19
Musil, Robert, 142
Mussolini, Benito, 3, 16, 157
  and Henry IV, 110
  and Pirandello, 15, 16, 17, 164
  myths and theater, 156, 157, 158

Naked. See To Clothe the Naked
naturalism, in *Six Characters*, 86, 89
Nazis, censorship by, 157
Neher, Caspar, 64–65
New Colony, The, 3, 156
New York *Morning Telegraph*
  review from, excerpted, 153
New York Post
  reviews from, excerpted, 58, 67, 101
New York Times
  reviews from, excerpted, 56, 67, 114–15, 116–17, 128, 152–53, 166
New York World-Telegram
  review from, excerpted, 167
Nobel Prize for Literature, 4, 19

Novelle per un anno, 3
Novel per Year, A, 3
novels, as drama, 24
Nuti, Baron, 129–42

Old and the Young, The, 2, 14
Olivieri, Egisto, 97
Outcast, The, 2

Pace, Madam, 76–101
Painful Joy, 1
Pallenberg, Max, 97
Picasso, Lamberto, 29, 96, 111–12
Piccolo Teatro (Milan), 61, 62, 164–65
Pinthus, Kurt, 97
Pirandello, Antonietta (wife), 2, 3, 7, 9–10, 80–81
Pirandello, Luigi
  as actor, 28–29
  biographical data of, 1–4
  and his daughter, 18, 80–81
  early career of, 18–21
  and his father, 7, 8–9
  influence of, 26
  lecture tours of, 4
  marriage of, 2, 3, 9–10, 80–81
  and politics, 10–18
  popularity of, 26–27, 141, 145
  quoted, 5, 8–9, 11, 13, 15, 17, 18, 40, 44, 139, 161
Pirandello, Stefano (father), 7–9, 13
Pirandello, Stefano (son), 44, 155, 166
Pitoëff, Georges, 113, 146
  productions by, 27, 78

play-within-the-play trilogy, 132, 144
Pleasure of Honesty, The,
68–75
productions of, 3, 69
synopsis of, 68–69
PM (newspaper)
review from, excerpted,
98
Polgar, Alfred, 74, 165
on Reinhardt, 149
politics and Pirandello, 10–
18
Ponza, Signor and Signora,
43–58, 67
Porter, Stephen, 58
Portulano, Antonietta. *See*
Pirandello, Anto-
nietta
Proctor, Buddy, illustration
of, 66
productions of the plays,
26–31
American, 55–58, 59, 66,
67, 78, 98, 100–101,
114–17, 128, 152–53,
166–67
comparisons of, 95–98
English, 78, 141
French, 78
German, 53–54, 60, 63,
64–65, 69, 78, 95–98,
98–100, 112–13, 141,
144–45, 155–56, 157,
165–66
illustrations of, 59–66
Italian, 27–30, 54–55, 61,
62, 69, 94–98, 111–12,
141–42, 155, 157
by Pirandello, 27–30, 54–
55, 69, 94–98, 111–12
by Reinhardt, 26, 27, 28,
95–98 passim

by Strehler, 62, 63, 155–
56, 164, 165–66
Professor Toti, 33
Provincetown Playhouse
(New York), 128
Puss in Boots (Tieck), 25

Rankin, Doris, illustration
of, 66
Rauhut, Franz, 161
Ravens of Misfortune, 154–
64
reality
and illusion, as theme,
102–111 passim
impossibility of, as
theater, 79–94 passim,
122, 132, 137, 150, 151
nature of, as theme, 45–53
search for, as theme, 118–
28 passim
and theater, 132, 140
*Rehearsal: Dramatic Scenes,
The*, 20
Reinhardt, Max, 146
dedication to, 145, 149
productions by, 26, 27, 28,
78, 95–98 passim
*Right You Are If You
Think You Are. See
Thus It Is*
Risorgimento, the, 12, 14
Robinson, Edward G., 56
illustration of, 59
Role Playing, 3
and *Six Characters*, 86
role playing, as theme, 24.
See also mask, the
Römische Elegien (Goethe),
1
Roundabout Theater (New
York), 58, 67

Russian theater, modern, 25, 146–47

Sampognetta, 143–53
Sands, Dorothy, 67
San Secondo, Russo di, 21
Sartre, Jean-Paul, 138
Schön, Gerhard, 99–100
Schuh, Oscar Fritz, 65, 98–99
Servaes, Franz, 98
Shaw, G. B., 78
Shepard, Lionel, 166
Shirley, Mercedes, 128
Shropshire, Anne, 128
Sicilian Limes, 2, 21
Sicily
    dialect theater of, 18–21
    as dramatic setting, 33–42 passim, 143–52 passim
    socialist uprising in, 2, 13–14
    society of, 5–10
Six Characters in Search of an Author, 19, 26, 28, 52, 69, 76–101, 103, 104, 111, 121, 123, 131, 132, 141, 145–46, 151, 152
    foreword to, 79, 80, 81, 90–91, 100
    and *Henry IV*, 105
    innovation in, 93
    origin of, 79–84
    popularity of, 26–27, 78
    productions of, 3, 27, 64–66, 78, 94–101
    synopsis of, 76–78
    and *To Clothe the Naked*, 119–20, 124
socialist uprising (Sicily), 2, 13–14

society. *See also* mass culture
    characters' adaptation to, 35–36, 41, 48–50, 71–73, 88, 106, 125, 137, 138–39
    as individuals, 135
    and Pirandello, 92, 140
    Sicilian, 5–10
    system of coercion of, 45–46, 109–110, 124–25, 126
Son, the, 76–101
Squarzina, Luigi, 141–42
staging, Pirandello on, 28–30
Stanislavsky method, 28
Stepdaughter, the, 76–101, 119–20
Strehler, Giorgio, productions by, 62, 63, 155–56, 164, 165–66
Strindberg, August, 104
    dramatic technique of, 159, 160
Su marito, 2
Sun (newspaper)
    review from, excerpted, 56–57
Suschka, Hurbert, illustration of, 60
Szoudi, Peter, 89

Tairov, Alexander, 146
Tallmer, Jerry, 58, 67
Teatro d'Arte di Roma, 3, 16, 27–30, 54–55, 69, 95, 146, 156
    tours of, 3, 16–17, 27–28, 69, 78, 94–95, 111
teatro-sul-teatro trilogy, 132, 144

theater
  conflict of, 84–85, 88–94,
    131–32, 151–52
  dialect, 18–21, 33, 44
  of the grotesque, 21–23,
    36
  modern Russian, 25, 146–
    47
  and myth, 156, 157, 158
  Pirandello's attitude to,
    19–21, 24, 149, 150–
    51, 156, 160–61
  and reality, 132, 140
  total, 146–47
Theater Guild (New York),
    55–56, 59
Theory of the Modern
    Drama (Szoudi), 89
Think, Giacomino!, 2, 19,
    21
Thus It Is (If It Seems So to
    You), 43–58, 67, 69
  innovations in, 45
  productions of, 2–3, 44,
    53–58, 59, 67
  synopsis of, 43–44
Tieck, Ludwig, 25
To Clothe the Naked, 118–
    28
  productions of, 3, 128
  and Six Characters, 119–
    20, 124
  synopsis of, 118–19
Tonight We Improvise, 4,
    132, 143–53
  productions of, 4, 144–45,
    152–53

  scandal over, 144–45
  synopsis of, 143–44
truth. See reality
Tynan, Kenneth, 115

umorismo, L', 2, 22–23
  quoted, 5, 11, 17
Upside-Down World
    (Tieck), 25

vecchi e i giovani, I, 2, 14
Vellinghausen, Albert
    Schulze, 113, 166
Verga, Giovanni, 17, 23
verismo, theme from, 146
Vilar, Jean, 113
Vise, The, 2, 20–21

Watt, Douglas, 67
Watts, Richard, 101
Weber, Carl, 114
Weiss, Rudolph, 128
Wiegler, Paul, 98
Williams, Clifford, 116
Williams, John S., 98
Wimmer, Maria, 165
  illustration of, 63

Yale School of Drama
    Repertory Theater,
    114–15
Yevreinov, Nikolai, 146
  dramaturgy of, 147
Young Pirandello, The
    (Rauhut), 161